TREKKING THE KUNGSLEDEN

About the Author

Mike Laing is a freelance mountaineering instructor based in Snowdonia, North Wales. He has travelled, climbed and trekked extensively in Greenland, South America, Africa, Europe and the Himalaya. This is his first guidebook for which he completed the Kungsleden as a through hike in 2017 and visited again twice in 2018 to complete and update his research. Mike is a full member of the Association of Mountaineering Instructors (AMI) and operates his own business, Snowdonia Climbing.

TREKKING THE KUNGSLEDEN

THE KING'S TRAIL THROUGH NORTHERN SWEDEN
by Mike Laing

JUNIPER HOUSE, MURLEY MOSS,
OXENHOLME ROAD, KENDAL, CUMBRIA LA9 7RL
www.cicerone.co.uk

© Mike Laing 2019
First edition 2019
ISBN: 978 1 85284 982 5

Printed in China on behalf of Latitude Press Ltd
A catalogue record for this book is available from the British Library.
All photographs are by the author unless otherwise stated.

Mapping by Lantmäteriet Sverige www.lantmateriet.se

Acknowledgements

*Special thanks are due to Steve Robertshaw of Visit Sweden and Eva
Gunnare for their generous and kind assistance with the glossary.*

Updates to this Guide

While every effort is made by our authors to ensure the accuracy of
guidebooks as they go to print, changes can occur during the lifetime of an
edition. Any updates that we know of for this guide will be on the Cicerone
website (www.cicerone.co.uk/982/updates), so please check before
planning your trip. We also advise that you check information about such
things as transport, accommodation and shops locally. Even rights of way
can be altered over time. We are always grateful for information about any
discrepancies between a guidebook and the facts on the ground, sent by
email to updates@cicerone.co.uk or by post to Cicerone, Juniper House,
Murley Moss, Oxenholme Road, Kendal, LA9 7RL.

Register your book: To sign up to receive free updates, special offers
and GPX files where available, register your book at www.cicerone.co.uk.

Front cover: Striding out on the open fell above Saltoluokta (Stage 9)

CONTENTS

Glacially polished rock (Stage 5)

Mountain safety

Walking in mountainous and remote areas has its dangers, and those regions described in this guidebook are no exception. All who walk or climb in the mountains should recognise this and take responsibility for themselves and their companions along the way. The author and publisher have made every effort to ensure that the information contained in this guide was correct when it went to press, but, except for any liability that cannot be excluded by law, they cannot accept responsibility for any loss, injury or inconvenience sustained by any person using this book.

International distress signal *(emergency only)*
Six blasts on a whistle (and flashes with a torch after dark) spaced evenly for one minute, followed by a minute's pause. Repeat until an answer is received. The response is three signals per minute followed by a minute's pause.

Helicopter rescue
The following signals are used to communicate with a helicopter:

Help needed:
raise both arms
above head to
form a 'Y'

Help not needed:
raise one arm
above head, extend
other arm downward

Emergency telephone numbers
Emergency service: 112
Non-emergency police support: 11414
Non-emergency health advice: 1177

Weather reports
There are no telephone weather services in Sweden that would be of use to walkers. All STF *fjällstugor* and *fjällstationer* have access to the latest forecasts and post these in communal areas. Even if you are not staying at STF facilities, the staff will be only too happy to provide the latest weather information as you pass through.

Mountain rescue can be very expensive – be adequately insured.

Route symbols on map extracts

〜 route

〜 alternative route

〜 link route

Ⓢ start point

Ⓕ finish point

ⓈⒻ start/finish point

▲ STF fjällstation/lodge

⬆ STF fjällstuga/hut

⬆ non-STF fjällstuga/hut

⬆ hostel/self-catering

Ⴟ campsite

■ railway station

▲ shelter/day hut

☏ Emergency telephone

GPX files
for all routes can be downloaded free at
www.cicerone.co.uk/982/GPX

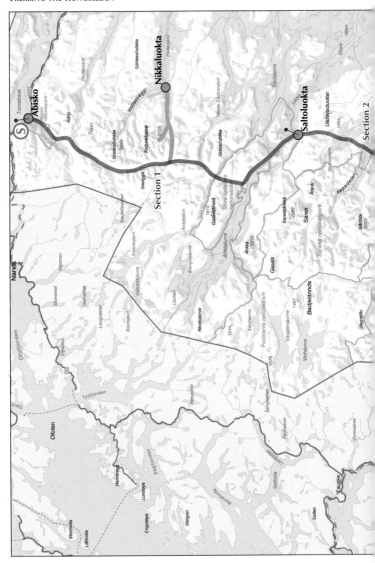

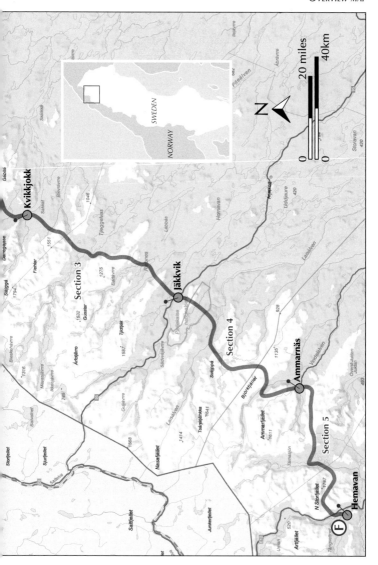

ROUTE SUMMARY TABLE

Stage		Distance (km)	Ascent/ Descent (m)	Time	Page
Section 1 – Abisko to Saltoluokta					**53**
Stage 1	Abisko to Abiskojaure	13.3	115/10	4hr 50min	60
Stage 2	Abiskojaure to Alesjaure	20.3	345/55	6hr 50min	67
Stage 3	Alesjaure to Tjäktja	13.1	265/30	4hr 45min	74
Stage 4	Tjäktja to Sälka	12.5	115/315	4hr 30min	79
Stage 5	Sälka to Singi	11.6	70/165	4hr 20min	85
Stage 6	Singi to Kaitumjaure	12.2	55/155	4hr 30min	90
Stage 7	Kaitumjaure to Teusajaure	8.6	200/320	3hr 30min	95
Stage 8	Teusajaure to Saltoluokta via Vakkotavare	13.7	480/510	4hr 50min	100
Total walking		*105.3*	*1645/1560*	*38hr 05min*	
Non-walking (boat crossings and bus)		*30.7*	*-*	*-*	
Section totals		*136*	*1645/1560*	*8 days*	
Section 2 – Saltoluokta to Kvikkjokk					**127**
Stage 9	Saltoluokta to Sitojaure	19.3	425/185	6hr 30min	131
Stage 10	Sitojaure to Aktse	8.3	325/395	3hr 20min	137
Stage 11	Aktse to Pårte	19.1	420/490	6hr 50min	144
Stage 12	Pårte to Kvikkjokk	15.2	90/260	5hr 20min	151
Total walking		*61.9*	*1260/1330*	*22hr*	
Non-walking (boat crossings)		*6.6*	*-*	*-*	
Section totals		*68.5*	*1260/1330*	*4 days*	
Section 3 – Kvikkjokk to Jäkkvik					**157**
Stage 13	Kvikkjokk to Tsielekjåhkå	11.9	480/190	4hr 30min	161
Stage 14	Tsielekjåhkå to Gistojávrátj	17.6	330/440	6hr	167
Stage 15	Gistojávrátj to Gásakláhko	19.7	540/150	6hr 40min	172
Stage 16	Gásakláhko to Vuonatjviken	12.9	20/400	4hr 40min	177
Stage 17	Vuonatjviken to Jäkkvik	16.4	435/515	5hr 40min	182
Total walking		*78.5*	*1805/1695*	*27hr 30min*	
Non-walking (boat crossings)		*9.1*	*-*	*-*	
Section totals		*87.6*	*1805/1695*	*5 days*	

Stage		Distance (km)	Ascent/ Descent (m)	Time	Page
Section 4 – Jäkkvik to Ammarnäs					**189**
Stage 18	Jäkkvik to Luvtávrre	13.2	450/290	4hr 45min	193
Stage 19	Luvtávrre to Bäverholmen	14.4	120/260	5hr	199
Stage 20	Bäverholmen to Tjiegnatisjávrrie	20	360/120	6hr 45min	205
Stage 21	Tjiegnatisjávrrie to Rävfalls	21.3	260/460	7hr	211
Stage 22	Rävfalls to Ammarnäs	22.2	490/570	7hr 20min	217
Section totals		*91.1*	*1680/1700*	*5 days (30hr 50min walking)*	
Section 5 – Ammarnäs to Hemavan					**225**
Stage 23	Ammarnäs to Aigert	7.4	390/20	3hr 10min	229
Stage 24	Aigert to Serve	19.2	575/655	6hr 30min	233
Stage 25	Serve to Tärnasjö	13.6	365/465	4hr 50min	238
Stage 26	Tärnasjö to Syter	14.2	135/35	5hr	242
Stage 27	Syter to Viterskals	12.4	280/190	4hr 30min	246
Stage 28	Viterskals to Hemavan	10.3	130/380	4hr	251
Section totals		*77.1*	*1875/1745*	*6 days (28hr walking)*	
Walking totals		**413.9**	**8265/8030**	**146hr 15min**	
Overall total		**460.3**	**8265/8030**	**146hr 15min**	

Note: Timings for bus and boat crossing have not been included in totals.

Additional itinerary 1 – Singi to Nikkaluokta					**107**
Day 1	Singi to Kebnekaise STF Fjällstation	14.1	200/260	5hr	108
Day 2	Kebnekaise STF Fjällstation to Nikkaluokta	17.9	130/310	6hr	114
Totals		*32*	*330/570*	*2 days (11hr walking)*	
Additional itinerary 2 – Kebnekaise summit					**120**
Kebnekaise STF Fjällstation to summit (round trip)		17.4	1720/1720	10hr	120

Crossing one of a number of bridges between Sälka and Singi (Stage 5)

INTRODUCTION

The Kaitumjåkka River seen from the south bank (Stage 7)

Sweden's Kungsleden (or King's Trail) embodies a diverse and unique walking experience whether it is taken in its entirety or just in part. Since its foundation in the early 20th Century by the Swedish Tourist Association (STF) the trail has grown and developed a section at a time from Abisko southwards to its current terminus in Hemavan, a total distance of 460km. For those visiting Sweden, Lappland and the Arctic for the first time the Kungsleden will be a grand adventure and a step into a new world; for many it will be the start of a long and rich association involving many repeated visits.

The Kungsleden is as varied as the Arctic wilderness is vast, traversing snow-topped mountain ranges, expansive open fell, verdant forests and crossing lakes both large and small. The trail begins by passing through the rugged Lapone Mountains, home to Kebnekaise, Sweden's highest peak at 2098m (which can be summitted by means of a detour from the Abisko to Nikkaluokta circuit – described in Additional itinerary 2). Like all long-distance trails the Kungsleden seeks the simplest line and in doing so traverses the Tjäktjavagge, a 30km glacial valley with magnificent views along its entire length. Further south the landscape softens to embrace open fell and the pristine lakes at Kaitumjaure and Teusajaure. At Aktse the famous hay meadows are perfectly framed by the azure Lájtávrre delta and the sheer chiselled face of Skierrffe. Beyond Kvikkjokk the trail becomes much quieter as it negotiates the empty fells and forest as far as Jäkkvik. On leaving Bäverholmen the trail climbs onto the Arjeplog Fells, an extensive and tranquil area much favoured by fishermen and naturalists alike. A brief and tantalising taste of Vindelälven precedes arrival into Ammarnäs, home to a beautiful amber coloured wooden church and the famous Potatisbacke (potato hill). On leaving Ammarnäs, open fells are followed as far as Tärnasjön lake after which the Kungsleden finishes as it started, among the mountains. Crossing the perfectly u-shaped Syterskalet valley places you within a day of Hemavan and the finish.

The Kungsleden is a continuous route with five distinct sections, allowing plenty of choice when it comes to how much of the trail you wish, or are able, to undertake. Many walkers limited by time spend a week walking the spectacular 103km from Abisko to Nikkaluokta (Stages 1–5, followed by Additional itinerary 1) through some of the Kungsleden's finest mountain scenery; an itinerary that includes the Tjäktjavagge. Those with more time can link multiple sections or even complete the entire trail, an undertaking requiring between four and five unhurried weeks for the average walker.

Despite the remoteness of the terrain, bridges are provided where needed by the Norrbotten and Västerbotten local councils, as are boardwalks across the roughest

Swedes in their element

and boggiest ground. Three of the Kungsleden's five sections are furnished with regular STF huts (*fjällstugor*) which offer a range of services and permit the weight-wary to walk with reduced loads. Most *fjällstugor* offer saunas which serve to ease aching muscles and reward you for your day's efforts. From start to finish the trail is very well marked and signposted making it straightforward to follow.

For half its length the Kungsleden lies within the Arctic Circle and consequently a large measure of the summer walking season takes place in 24-hour daylight. This is also Sápmi, home of the Sámi people whose close relationship with the reindeer has underpinned their existence since the last ice age. The reindeer are mostly absent during the walking season, although the Sámi are evidenced by their summer villages, their traditional dwellings (*kåtor*), reindeer enclosures (*rengärden*) and remote huts.

Lappland is home to a remarkable group of animals including brown bear, wolverine, arctic fox, moose and many others; all are wary of humans and a sighting from the trail is unlikely. As compensation there are many eye-catching Arctic plants to enjoy (and berries to eat) as well as waterfowl and other bird types; if you're lucky you might catch a glimpse of otter, lemming and moose. Along its length the Kungsleden passes through no fewer than five national parks including Sarek whose beautiful snowy mountains provide a spectacular sight in the distance.

Sweden's *allemansrätten* (everyman's right) allows great freedom to roam in the outdoors and to wild camp, light fires, pick berries and swim in the lakes. This is all part of the joy of the Kungsleden and what makes it such a special experience. You will encounter many Swedes on the trail and their cheerful, friendly and open company does much to enrich the overall experience, as does that of the small communities encountered along the way.

So, this is Sweden's Kungsleden, a colourful, rugged, varied, magnificent and remote walking experience. Although the vast majority of the route is very quiet, certain parts of the trail will feel busy or crowded to some walkers. Luckily, an antidote can be found by camping in the many tranquil spots found along the way. Whatever your level of ability and experience the Kungsleden offers numerous options and a great deal for everyone to enjoy and appreciate.

THE SUBARCTIC ENVIRONMENT

Geography

Sweden has an area of 450,000km^2 making it the fourth-largest country entirely in Europe. Around 65 per cent of this area is covered in forest and 9 per cent in water. Northern Sweden (or Lappland) provides a spectacular

Skierffe reveals itself on the descent to Aktse (Stage 10)

landscape of forest, lake, tundra and mountains.

Some 15 per cent of Sweden's total landmass lies within the Arctic Circle and experiences the splendour of 24-hour daylight in the midsummer and 24-hour darkness in midwinter. Due to its latitude, Arctic Sweden experiences long deep winters and brief abundant summers.

Over a cycle of 40,000 years the latitude of the Arctic Circle fluctuates by as much as 2° as a result of changes in the Earth's axial tilt. At present the Arctic Circle is moving northwards at a rate of approximately 15m a year, or about a kilometre in a lifetime.

At present the Arctic Circle lies at a latitude of 66°33′46.5″ north and intersects the Kungsleden approximately 20km north of Jäkkvik. The long arctic winter locks Lappland in darkness, snow, ice and sub-zero temperatures. Spring comes slow and late and is accompanied by the melt which swells rivers and makes crossings hazardous; on higher ground and in shaded corners the snow recedes but never disappears. In the brief hiatus of summer indigenous life must be vigorous and make the most of the short season.

Climate

Sweden benefits from a much milder climate than most other regions that lie so far north, such as Greenland. This is due to the moderating influence of the Gulf Stream, a warm ocean current that flows off Norway's west coast. The predominant air mass affecting Sweden is continental, a type that brings stable high pressure weather systems. In summer this results in hot dry conditions accompanied by mild winds, and in winter, biting cold temperatures. This stability is disturbed by less stable, moist, low pressure weather systems arriving from the Atlantic on the Gulf Stream which serve to moderate the extremes of temperature in both summer and winter. In summer the low pressure systems serve to increase precipitation, produce locally stronger winds and lower the temperatures. Summer weather will therefore depend on the type of weather system that is prevailing at any given time. Temperatures in Lappland are regionally depressed by the high subarctic and Arctic latitudes. It is because of these high latitudes that the northern areas of the province experience midnight sun in the summer and a polar night with some civil twilight during the winter.

While on the trail in summer you can expect predominantly high pressure weather systems bringing stable weather, although low temperatures, rainfall and challenging weather can occur at any time; storms can blow in very quickly in the mountains encountered on Sections 1 and 5 of the trail. The prevalent wind direction is from the south west and these will be mainly light, although fresher on the open fell. Air temperatures fall close to or below the dew point on many nights which may result in condensation issues for those camping.

Average annual precipitation for Abisko is 387mm, with July the wettest month, receiving an average of 59mm. Hemavan in contrast receives almost twice the annual precipitation of Abisko with 774mm; July is again the wettest month with an average of 88mm. Historical climate graphs for all section termini can be viewed at Weather Underground (www. wunderground.com/history).

Average length of day (hours)												
	Jan	Feb	Mar	Apr	May	Jun	Jul	Aug	Sep	Oct	Nov	Dec
Kvikkjokk	6	9	13	17	21	24	22	19	14	10	7	4

Average min/max temperature (°C)												
	Jan	Feb	Mar	Apr	May	Jun	Jul	Aug	Sep	Oct	Nov	Dec
Abisko	-13/-6	-12/-5	-10/-2	-5/2	0/8	5/13	8/16	7/14	3/9	-2/3	-8/-2	-11/-5
Kvikkjokk	-15/-7	-14/-5	-10/-1	-5/3	0/9	6/15	8/17	7/15	3/10	-1/4	-8/-2	-13/-5
Hemavan	-11/-4	-10/-3	-8/0	-4/4	1/9	5/14	8/16	7/15	4/10	0/5	-5/0	-9/-3

Average precipitation (mm)/number of days with precipitation												
	Jan	Feb	Mar	Apr	May	Jun	Jul	Aug	Sep	Oct	Nov	Dec
Kvikkjokk	42/11	33/9	31/9	29/6	36/6	57/9	87/12	76/11	63/9	55/10	47/11	47/11

Geology

Sweden lies within the Eurasian tectonic plate and is thus relatively stable. This does not mean there is no activity. On Saturday 19 March 2016 Sweden experienced its strongest tremor in 100 years when a 4.2 magnitude earthquake was recorded in the Gulf of Bothnia by the European-Mediterranean Seismological Centre (EMSC).

Within the Eurasian Plate, Sweden is part of the Fennoscandian Shield, a zone of very old Pre-Cambrian crystalline and metamorphic rocks which have consolidated during hundreds of millions of years; the oldest being about three billion years old. Common rock types are gneiss, granite, granodiorite, sandstone and marble. Over this bedrock lies the drift which is the product of numerous periods of glaciation and deglaciation. The most common soil type is glacial till that covers about 75 per cent of the landscape.

Much of the bedrock in Lappland is crystalline, resistant to weathering and non-porous; as a result the soil and plant covering is generally thin. The spring thaw causes dramatic water runoff which, when combined with a harsh climate, makes for a challenging growing environment. It is the combination of these factors that leads to the fells being devoid of any substantial tree and forest growth on ground found above the sheltered valley floors. The action of glaciation over millions of years has carved magnificent and steep-sided u-shaped valleys, resulting in a wonderful landscape for walkers to explore.

Micro-folded rock

PLANTS AND ANIMALS

Surviving the Arctic environment has required millennia of adaptation and tenacity from all forms of life be it plant, animal or human. Many of the native animals hibernate or migrate for the winter. Those that stay eke it out on the very margins of survival while the plant life lies dormant under the snow. It is during the brief summer months and the walking season that there is the greatest opportunity to see and experience the region's plants and animals.

Mammals

Sweden's 'Big Four' are the lynx (*lodjur*), wolverine (*järv*), brown bear (*brun björn*) and wolf (*varg*) although unfortunately, not all are now to be found on the Kungsleden, the wolf having been largely driven out by Sámi reindeer herding. As noted, such species are very wary of humans and the chance of seeing any of them is slim. You may be lucky and catch a fleeting glimpse of the common otter (*utter*) by a remote stream and also possibly moose (*älg*), especially at the start of Stage 7 and the second day of Additional itinerary 1. Wild camping is more likely to bring the walker into contact with animals than staying in or near a *stuga*, the exception being at Tjäktja. Dawn and dusk will be the best time for observing and if particularly interested, you may wish to carry a lightweight pair of binoculars. Tjäktja has a reputation for sightings of the more exotic species such as wolverine and Arctic fox (*fjällräv*). Generally speaking, transition zones between different habitats are good places to observe animals, examples being where forest and open fell meet or along water edges. Lemming (*fjällämmel*) are often seen scurrying around beneath the wooden boardwalks.

Reindeer (*ren*) will be encountered although in summer most will have migrated westwards seeking higher and cooler ground near the Norwegian border. Here they remain until they migrate back eastwards in search of mushrooms to supplement their diet. Both sexes grow and shed antlers annually.

Birds

There will be opportunities for seeing raptors so keep a good lookout for golden eagles (*kungsörn*) and white-tailed eagles (*vit-tailed örn*) soaring on high or peregrines (*pilgrimsfalk*) diving from the high cliffs on Sections 1 and 5. Willow grouse (*dalripa*) and snow bunting (*snösparv*) are, however, much more likely companions, along with bluethroat (*blåhake*), red poll (*gråsiska*) and arctic tern (*arktiska tärna*). The Swedish ornithological society is the Sveriges Ornitologiska Förening (www.birdlife.se – Swedish only).

Fish

Some walkers may want to fish, especially as the lakes and rivers are generally abundant with species such as arctic char (*röding*), grayling (*harr*), salmon (*lax*) and brown trout (*brun forell*). Fishing permits (*fiskekort*) are required and can be obtained from tourist information, shops and some STF *fjällstugor* and *fjällstationer*. *Fiskekort* generally cost SEK50 to SEK200 per day depending on the exact location and season.

Plants and flowers

Much will be seen of the birch (*björk*) on the Kungsleden, in the birch and mixed forests but also dwarf birch out on the open fell. Dwarf willow (*vide*) varieties are also common and distinguished one from the other by their leaf shape.

A bonus is that some of the plant species have edible berries and foraging is permitted as a right in *allemansrätten*. Spoils will be much better a short distance from the trail as the best will already have been picked by previous walkers. Keep an eye open for blueberry (*blåbär*) and crowberry (*kråkbär*) which grows very close to the ground and looks near black in colour. The crowberry is smaller than the blueberry and bittier in the mouth; they are best eaten by the handful and chewed for their juice, spitting out the bits once done. Lingonberries (*lingon*) are common, although sharp and bitter. Look out for the cloudberry

(*hjörtron*) which is a tangy and flavoursome fruit thriving on marshy ground. It ripens between the end of July and the middle of August and is best eaten when an orange/yellow colour. Although poisonous species are rare, make certain you have identified any foraged food before eating – especially mushrooms.

The short Arctic summer produces a colourful display of alpine and Arctic flowers, generally small in stature but no less attractive for this; identification is aided by posters in the *fjällstugor*. Common species are the delicate arctic harebell (*blåklocka*), *Kung Karls spira*, *torta*, *mossljung*, *hönsbär*, buttercup (*smörblomma*), *smörboll*, *gullbräcka* and a number of orchid species such as the heath

Crowberry (top L); Lingon (R); Juniper (bottom L);

(Top row, from L) Hönsbär; Kung Karls spira; Nordisk Stormhatt
(Bottom row) Arctic harebell *(blåklocka)*; Kråkklöver

spotted-orchid *(jungfru Marie nycklar)*. A small pocket guide to the *fjällblommor* (fell flowers) is available at *fjällstationer* and tourist information or, if you are starting in Hemavan, a visit to the Naturum/Fjällbotaniska exhibition centre will be very informative.

REGIONAL HISTORY

Sweden's story began, as did that of many other nations, at the end of the last ice age about 12,000 years ago when rising temperatures caused the ice to retreat and life to venture in. Among the first arrivals were herds of reindeer which were hotly pursued by the Komsa, a late-Palaeolithic/early-Mesolithic hunter-gatherer people whose existence is evidenced by petroglyphs and other archaeological relics dating back to this period. There are striking similarities between the decorative patterns found on Komsa bone artefacts and those used by the later Sámi which has led anthropologists to conclude a cultural continuity between the two cultures. The Sámi,

23

who survive and thrive to this day, lived and worked a vast area that stretched over the northern parts of present-day Norway, Sweden, Finland and the Russian Kola Peninsula for at least 5000 years; a region known as Sápmi (Lapland). The part of Sweden that is home to the Sámi (which forms part of the greater Sápmi) is referred to as Lappland.

The Sámi pursued a variety of livelihoods including coastal fishing, fur trapping, and sheep herding. But the Sámi are renowned for their relationship with the plentiful reindeer that roamed Sápmi. For millennia this association was one of hunter and hunted until dwindling stocks in the 17th century forced the Sámi to adopt the lifestyle seen to this day – that of semi-nomadic reindeer herders. About

10 per cent of the estimated 30,000 Sámi living in Sweden are still directly connected to reindeer herding in some way, with the animals providing meat, fur, and transportation. Some 2800 Sámi are still actively involved in herding on a full-time basis, and the Sámi hold sole rights to the pursuit of reindeer husbandry in Sweden.

While the Sámi pursued their hunter-gatherer lifestyle in the north, Bronze and Iron Age cultures flourished to the south. Eventually a powerful new people arrived, the Svea, who spread and occupied much of what is now Sweden. There was much inter-tribal feuding but by the 6th century the Svea of the Mälaren Valley had gained ascendancy and it is their dominion, Svea Rike, that gave Sweden its name, Sverige.

Between the late 8th and mid-11th centuries the Vikings held sway, especially on the sea. While the reputation of these Norsemen was fierce, the Swedish variety were more given to commerce than their Danish and Norwegian cousins. The key to the Vikings' success was their rugged, manoeuvrable and fast longboats. Using these vessels they ventured as far as Greenland, Newfoundland, Istanbul and Baghdad, all the time establishing trade links. The paganism practised by the Vikings held sway until the arrival of Christianity around the first millennium.

A lack of reliable evidence makes it difficult to say who the first king of Sweden was. Most lists of succession begin in the 10th century with King Olof Skötkonung and his father Eric the Victorious; King Eric (c. 970–995) is the first Swedish king about whom anything definite is known. Whether or not he qualified as King of Sweden is still debated as it is King Olof who is recorded as the first ruler to have been accepted both by the Svea and Götar peoples. Both father and son were the first Swedish Kings to be baptised.

Sweden finally emerged as an independent and unified country during the Middle Ages and in the 17th century it expanded its territories to form the Swedish Empire, emerging as one of the great powers of Europe. However, from the early 18th century onwards, territories outside the Scandinavian Peninsula were gradually lost and the empire fell into decline, ending with the annexation of present-day Finland by Russia in 1809. The last war in which Sweden was directly involved was in 1814 when Norway was militarily forced into a union. Since then Sweden has been at peace and has maintained an official policy of neutrality in foreign affairs. The union with Norway was peacefully dissolved in 1905, establishing Sweden's current borders.

The 18th and 19th centuries saw a significant population increase, attributed by the writer Esaias Tegnérin to 'the peace, the smallpox vaccine, and the potato': between 1750 and 1850, the population of Sweden doubled. According to some, mass emigration to America became the only way to prevent famine and rebellion and the 1880s saw an annual emigration rate of more than one per cent. It is believed that between 1850 and 1910 more than one million Swedes emigrated to America.

Sweden remained impoverished, retaining a largely agricultural economy even as Denmark and Western European countries began to industrialise. However, despite the slow rate of industrialisation into the 19th century, many important changes were taking place in the agrarian economy due to innovation and the rapid population growth; innovations such as government-sponsored programmes of enclosure, aggressive exploitation of agricultural lands, and the introduction of new crops such as the potato. Providentially, feudalism and serfdom had never been a part of Swedish life and the farming community was sufficiently emancipated to begin taking on a critical role in Swedish politics. This has continued through to the present day with the Agrarian Party.

It wasn't until between 1870 and 1914 that Sweden began to develop the modern industrialised economy that exists today. Modern Sweden is a constitutional monarchy and a parliamentary democracy: legislative power is vested in the 349-member Riksdag while executive power is exercised by the government chaired by the prime minister. Sweden joined the European Union on 1 January 1995, but declined NATO membership as well as Eurozone membership following a referendum.

Sweden maintains a Nordic social welfare system that provides universal health care and tertiary education for its citizens. It has the world's eighth-highest per capita income and ranks highly in numerous metrics of national performance including, among others, quality of life, protection of civil liberties and equality.

The Kungsleden crosses Lappland and therefore you will come into contact with Sámi culture; most of the geographic terms and labels on the mapping are in Sámi, not Swedish. The Sámi have never been a single community in a single region. In an all-too-familiar tale the Sámi were for centuries the subject of discrimination and abuse by dominant cultures which claimed possession of their land rights, although governments have in recent times sought to officially recognise

Handelsbod from the outside (Stage 19)

Ammarnäs framed by a rainbow en route to Aigert (Stage 23)

and protect Sámi culture – to some degree. Sweden recognised the existence of the 'Sámi nation' in 1989, but the UN International Labour Organisation's Indigenous and Tribal Peoples Convention C169 was not adopted and all indigenous rights are currently banned. The Sametingslag was established as the Swedish Sámi Parliament on 1 January 1993. In 1998 the Swedish government formally apologised for the wrongs committed against the Sámi. At present, although the Swedish Compulsory School Ordinance states that Sámi pupils are entitled to be taught in their native language, a municipality is only obliged to provide Sámi-medium education if a suitable teacher is available and the pupil has a basic knowledge of Sámi.

WHEN TO GO

Although the Kungsleden is traversed during winter by skiers and those on snow mobiles, this guidebook concerns itself solely with summer trekking. Walking the trail, even if you intend to wild camp, is only practical when the STF *fjällstugor* (mountain huts) and *fjällstationer* (mountain stations) are open. This is generally mid-June till the end of September with the exact dates for each year publicised on the STF website. It is only during this period that the STF rowing boats will be in place at their crossings and that the motorised boat services, both STF and private, will be operating. Any earlier and there will be too much deep snow on the trail and the streams and rivers will still be swollen with meltwater, any later and the temperatures will be falling fast and the first winter snows arriving.

Much of the trail is within the Arctic Circle and there are long periods when 24-hour daylight prevails. This may make for unhurried walking days but it will not suit everyone. A good resource for calculating day length (for all dates and latitudes) is www.suncalc.net. If you are a light sleeper or you feel you will not be able sleep when it is light, then it would be sensible to plan your walk during the parts of the season that do not experience 24-hour daylight.

One particular period in which to avoid Section 1 is the third week in August when thousands flock onto the trail between Abisko and Nikkaluokta to take part in the Fjällräven Classic, a mass participation trek organised by the clothing and gear manufacturer (http://classic.fjallraven.com/sweden). For those walking Additional itinerary 1, it may be worth noting that Kebnekaise Fjällstation can get very hectic at weekends. The busiest period on the trail is the final week in July and the first two weeks in August when the majority of Swedes take their summer holiday.

Poor weather and insects are not side-stepped with any certainty. Those wishing to avoid the insects should aim for the very opening and close of the summer season. Otherwise, and especially if wild camping, your choice of site will be critical; above the treeline, away from standing water and where there is a breeze. Weather

in the mountains and on the fell can be fickle at any time in the summer, although walking at the season's extremes is certainly more prone to cooler conditions and less predictable weather. Much of the summer is 24-hour daylight, meaning there is no possibility of seeing the aurora borealis. However, at the very start and finish of the summer season when it does get dark, it is possible to see the aurora on clear nights.

PLANNING YOUR WALK

The overriding factor for most walkers will be the amount of time they have available. Walking the entire Kungsleden end to end takes over four weeks, assuming a couple of the shorter stages are combined and a day or two kept in hand for rest days and any unforeseen delays. Those unable to commit for this long will be constrained to undertaking a limited number of sections, completing the trail over a number of visits or taking some shortcuts such as those on stages 21 and 23 which miss out Rävfalls and Aigert.

A key consideration is how much use you will make of the *fjällstugor* and *fjällstationer*. Those choosing to wild camp, be it for esoteric or budgetary reasons, are likely to make little or no call on their facilities. While the *fjällstugor* and *fjällstationer* are expensive, they do offer reassurance to some walkers and also a substantial weight saving in terms of equipment that needs not be carried; food, stove, fuel, tent, sleeping bag and roll mat.

For those on a budget, another way to keep costs down is to make full use of the STF rowing boats where they are supplied, although this will slow your progress.

Are you going to factor in rest days? Are you going to need them? Jäkkvik, Adolfsström and Ammarnäs are all beautiful and tempting places to stop for a day or two, to rest, resupply and discover the local area.

In which direction will you travel? Most walkers, especially those through-hiking, travel from north to south along the trail. This is a particularly good choice if you are walking at the season's end as winter comes sooner to the north than it does to the south. Southwards is also the manner in which the Kungsleden evolved over time and it seems a natural and popular way to travel. Walking northwards has its merits, especially at the season's start and, for the reverse reasons stated for heading south at the season's end. Heading northwards will place the sun at your back, which will aid photography and also maximise the efficiency of any solar charging device being carried on your rucksack. Finally, those walking northwards are more likely to find two rowing boats waiting for them at crossings and are therefore less likely to have to make three crossings in order to return a boat. Both Section

Walkers on Stage 8; Lunch stop on the trail; Walker on Stage 8

1 and 5 have dramatic mountainous landscapes, meaning that both directions have starts and finishes that are of a similar character and difficulty.

TRANSPORT

The Kungsleden has a reputation for being challenging to access and travel around, and to some extent this is true given the remoteness of the region. Walkers are advised to research their travel options fully as onward connections in more remote areas are not always daily or frequent. While the Kungsleden's extremities at Abisko and Hemavan are readily accessed, getting to and from the intermediate sections is more complex and requires careful research. The greatest transport challenges will be faced by those planning to walk non-consecutive sections, while through-hikers will benefit from very good transport links at their start and finish.

There are a number of useful websites (nearly all with associated apps) that simplify travel planning. An invaluable tool is the Swedish Railways (SJ) website (www.sj.se/en/home.html) which includes comprehensive railway information and allows cross-modal enquiries and bookings to be made including a combination of rail and bus legs. Note that itineraries and bookings may only be made three months in advance. For local bus services the Länstrafiken Norrbotten (www.ltnbd.se/en/timetables) and Länstrafiken Västerbotten (www.tabussen.nu/lanstrafiken/english) websites provide travel information for their respective counties. Resrobot (www.resrobot.se/#plan – Swedish only) is another multi-modal travel resource as is Google Maps' Go function although the former is now starting to show its age.

Kiruna, Umeå and Narvik are served by SAS Airlines (www.flysas.com/en/uk) or Norwegian Air (www.norwegian.com/uk) although Narvik only has direct flights to Oslo and requires at least one change to reach Stockholm. As of May 2018, Next Jet, which served Hemavan, Lycksele, Arvidsjaur and Gällivare, ceased operating. Estonian airline Nordica (www.nordica.ee/en/home) now serves Arvidsjaur and Gällivare although Hemavan and Lycksele, at the time of

The second of the seven bridges on Stage 26

Transport to the Kungsleden

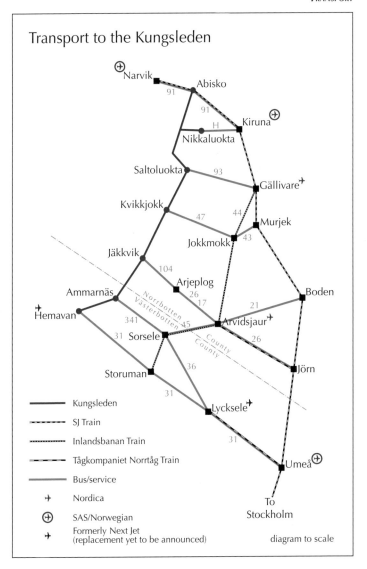

- —— Kungsleden
- ⊶⊶⊶ SJ Train
- ⋯⋯ Inlandsbanan Train
- ⊷⊷ Tågkompaniet Norrtåg Train
- —— Bus/service
- ✈ Nordica
- ⊕ SAS/Norwegian
- ✈ Formerly Next Jet
  (replacement yet to be announced)

diagram to scale

31

writing, are still without scheduled air links in or out.

Getting to the route

Travelling around the Kungsleden can seem daunting, although the good news is that it needn't be. Plan well in advance, make good use of the online tools and things will start to seem clearer and more simple. Incorporating a little wiggle room into your travel plans will prevent a missed connection becoming a crisis. Linking non-consecutive sections of the trail is not easy and will require careful planning; the key to success will be good use of the hubs and travelling with the information already to hand – i.e. not relying on internet connectivity for your information while on the trail.

Kiruna is the hub for **Abisko** and **Nikkaluokta** in the north. Daily SAS and Norwegian flights link Stockholm and Kiruna from where there is a choice of bus or SJ train for onwards travel to Abisko and bus for Nikkaluokta. A popular alternative to flying is the daily (direct) 17-hour overnight SJ train from Stockholm (the Arctic Circle Train). This offers reasonably priced seats and couchettes and stops at both Kiruna and Abisko the next morning; sufficiently early to start the trail. There are additional SJ train services from Stockholm that involve changes and different arrival times into Kiruna and Abisko. From Kiruna, Nikkaluokta is accessed via the privately operated Hörvalls Nikkaluoktaexpressen bus service

(www.horvalls.se – Swedish only); travel time is 1hr 15min.

Gällivare, the hub for **Saltoluokta** and **Vakkotavare**, is served by near daily flights from Stockholm operated by Nordica. Another option is the aforementioned overnight SJ train from Stockholm which stops at Gällivare and will allow you to catch the 93 bus onwards to Saltoluokta and Vakkotavare. **Kvikkjokk** can also be accessed from Gällivare via the 44 then the 47 bus which adds up to over five hours of travel. Another option is again to take the overnight SJ train from Stockholm but disembark at Murjek from where the 43 and 47 buses will take you to Kvikkjokk via Jokkmokk in about five hours.

Arvidsjaur serves as the hub for **Jäkkvik** mid-trail and is served by near daily flights from Stockholm operated by Nordica. Again, SJ train is an option for reaching Arvidsjaur with the overnight SJ train from Stockholm calling at Jörn from where Arvidsjaur is reached on the 26 bus in an hour, or connecting Tågkompaniet Norrtåg train in three hours; those alighting at Boden can catch the 21 bus for the two-hour journey to Arvidsjaur. From Arvidsjaur, Jäkkvik is another two bus rides (17 or 26 followed by the 104 services) and four-and-a-half hours away.

Arvidsjaur can also be used to reach **Ammarnäs** via a combination of Inlandsbanan regional train (www.inlandsbanan.se/en) or 45 bus to Sorsele followed by the onward

341 bus. The overnight SJ train from Stockholm will get you to Umeå by around 06.20 from where the 31, 36 and 341 buses in turn would see you in Ammarnäs six hours later, luck permitting.

Hemavan is linked to Umeå by the 31 bus (five-and-a-half hours). From Umeå, SAS/Norwegian flights or SJ train can be used for onward travel to Stockholm. At present no scheduled flights serve Hemavan.

BOAT CROSSINGS

There are seven mandatory boat crossings to make on the Kungsleden, along with four optional crossings. These add colour and enhance the adventure of the walking experience and have been very much part of the

Kungsleden's heritage since its inception. Current information and tariffs can be found on a dedicated STF webpage (www.swedishtouristassociation.com/learn/boats-in-the-mountains).

Four of the seven mandatory crossings are furnished with STF rowing boats and all but one (the shortest) of the seven also have a motorised pay service. There is no charge for using the rowing boats but it does take time and there may be a queue in peak season, meaning an extended wait. Rowed crossings are equipped with three rowing boats, the minimum required to guarantee both shores have a boat available at any one time. When you have completed your row across you must ensure each shore has a boat waiting for other walkers. If this is not the case you must return

STF rowing boats, Teusajaure Lake crossing (Stage 7)

towing a second boat, leave it on the far shore and row back again. Thus you may end up making the crossing three times. At Sitojaure and Lájtávrre this would mean at least 9km of rowing! Rowing boats are stored on racks on the shore and should be left as found. Life jackets are provided. The rowing boats are in situ for summer then withdrawn and put into storage when the STF *fjällstugor* and *fjällstationer* close. If you are unsure about your rowing prowess a short practise close to the shore should be of benefit and keep you out of trouble. Full details on the nuances of each crossing are contained in the relevant stage descriptions and a summary of all crossings is in Appendix C.

Although most motorised services are STF operated, some are privately run and therefore the price for crossings varies, from SEK100 to SEK350. On Section 3 between Kvikkjokk and Jäkkvik, pre-arranging the crossing of Riebnes Lake could save you many hours of waiting, especially at the very start or end of the season.

ACCOMMODATION

All section ends have accommodation available, be it an STF *fjällstation*, self-catering, hostel or hotel. Appendix A summarises all the non-emergency facilities encountered from the Kungsleden's start in Abisko to the finish in Hemavan.

STF fjällstugor and fjällstationer
Three of the Kungsleden's five sections (1, 2 and 5) are fully furnished with

Typical fjällstuga interior

STF *fjällstugor*. Facilities vary between *stugor* although all provide beds, self-catering facilities and camping as a minimum, most have a *bastu* (sauna) and a shop as well. Sleeping in the *fjällstugor* is not cheap, but it does negate the need for camping equipment and means walkers can travel light and fast. Note that a sleeping bag liner is required. Camping at the *fjällstugor* is much cheaper and still grants access to the facilities on site. STF members and affiliates pay lower rates than non-members and also benefit from free daytime access when passing through, non-members pay a notional fee for day visitor benefits. Savings for STF members are substantial, and only a few days spent in a hut will recoup the cost of membership. All *fjällstugor* and *fjällstationer* accept Swedish krona cash.

Although not essential, advance booking a bed online is cheaper than just turning up. It should be noted however that a booking is only a proof of payment and does not guarantee a bed; beds are issued on a first-come-first-served basis on the day. Nevertheless, no one is turned away if beds are filled, mattresses and bedding will be provided for any overflow. The advantage of this system is that a booking doesn't restrict you to the date or the *fjällstuga* you have booked and your booking can be used at any *fjällstuga* on any date within the season. In this respect the online booking is more like a voucher. Rather generously, cancellation and refund is available until the day before the chosen start date; after this, no refunds will be made. Walkers are advised to carry proof of booking. Camping at *fjällstugor* and *fjällstationer* does not require pre-booking. Detailed information on every *fjällstuga* and *fjällstation*, up-to-date prices and seasonal dates can be found on the STF website (www.swedishtouristassociation. com).

STF *fjällstationer* are located at Abisko, Kebnekaise, Saltoluokta, Kvikkjokk, Ammarnäs and Hemavan, the latter two being STF affiliated. These are much bigger than the *fjällstugor* and offer full facilities such as running water, parcel collection, restaurant, electricity, Wi-Fi and a large shop. Bookings at *fjällstationer*, unlike those at *fjällstugor*, are non-transferrable and do guarantee a bed on the date booked.

As of 2019 prices are SEK350 for an adult STF member pre-booking a bed at a *fjällstuga*, SEK450 for a non-member. Section 1 as far south as Singi attracts a higher tariff than the rest of the Kungsleden – SEK450 and SEK550 respectively. Prices for under-16s are a very reasonable SEK0 (free) and SEK150 respectively across the entire Kungsleden. Camping fees at *fjällstugor* are SEK180 and SEK280 respectively. STF membership cost SEK295 for over-25s, SEK150 for 16-25-year-olds, and SEK30 for under 16s, family membership is SEK450 (two adults, with all children and young people registered at the same

Examples of STF fjällstugor *and* fjällstationer *emblems*

address). Membership can be purchased online or on the trail at *fjällstationer* and *fjällstugor*. Those holding a

Hostelling International card receive reciprocal membership rights with the STF.

All STF *fjällstugor* and *fjällsta-tioner* have their own unique emblem. These can be purchased as sew-on cloth badges with a green border for summer and a blue border for winter. *Stugvärdar* (hut wardens) also have an ink stamp which can be used to decorate guidebooks if so desired.

Camping

Allemansrätten allows the public to camp overnight and, with the exception of the Abisko National Park on Stage 1, you are at liberty to wild camp anywhere along the Kungsleden. Those choosing to camp will enjoy maximum freedom on the trail but still be able to use *fjällstuga* facilities for *bastu* (sauna), as day visitors passing through, for resupply, camping or even sleeping inside occasionally. Good camping is not be found

everywhere however, and forests generally provide limited camping opportunities. Information contained in the stage descriptions and maps should ensure that those camping always find themselves a good site.

Other

Section 3 between Kvikkjokk and Jäkkvik is the least well provided section with respect to accommodation, there being but one small and basic unmanned STF *fjällstuga* at Tsielekjåkkå. Despite this, the section is just traversable without a tent if Tsielekjåkkå is used, followed by a 29km walk to the very basic *kåta* on Stage 15, followed by a 20km walk to Vuonatjviken where there is self-catering accommodation readily available. The final day will see you safely in Jäkkvik. You should only consider going without a tent on Section 3 if you are certain you can cover the distances; food, stove and a sleeping bag will still be required.

Although Section 4 between Jäkkvik and Ammarnäs has no STF facilities, there are a number of options for accommodation at Pieljekaise (unmanned *stuga*), Adolfsström (self-catering), Bäverholmen (self-catering), Snjulttjie (unmanned and very basic cabin) and Rävfallsstugan (unmanned *stuga*). These facilities allow you to cross the section without a tent; the longest walk between accommodation being the 27.3km from Snjulttjie to Rävfallsstugan. Both Pieljekaise and Rävfallsstugan are operated by the local council and require you to collect the keys to gain full access to the facilities; full details are provided

in the text. As for Section 3, sleeping bag, stove and food will be required.

Emergency shelters

There are a number of emergency shelters on the trail which make for good rest stops, especially in poor weather. While you are welcome to stop, rest and shelter, overnighting is prohibited in such shelters except in the event of an emergency. Emergency stores such as emergency wood and *nödlåda* (emergency boxes) found on site should also only be used in an emergency.

HUT LIFE AND FACILITIES

The STF *fjällstugor* enable access to many walkers who wouldn't otherwise venture onto the Kungsleden. The *stugor* provide shelter, accommodation,

The idyllic Bárasjuhka emergency shelter (Stage 20)

Stugvärdar at Aktse (Stage 10)

food, resupply, drying rooms, fellowship and reassurance in areas that are devoid of habitation and services.

In all, there are 16 STF *fjällstugor* on the Kungsleden, all regularly spaced along Sections 1, 2 and 5. These are manned by volunteer *stugvärdar* who are without exception, welcoming and helpful. The *stugvärdar* spend between five and six weeks at their *stuga* and can, at larger *stugor*, bring their family along if they wish. All receive specific training at Abisko Fjällstation prior to the season's start before packing a box of belongings and all the food for their upcoming tenure. These boxes are transported out with the firewood stores, towed by skidoos during the hiatus between winter and summer seasons. The provision of firewood

is by far the largest cost to the STF of running remote *stugor*. *Stugvärdar* are not salaried but are paid a small allowance to cover the running costs they are still accruing at home.

All the *stugor* are positioned directly on the trail and consist of a cluster of wooden cabins and outbuildings. All have dorm rooms with beds and bedding, sometimes there will be a wood stove in the dorm. There will also be a communal cooking and dining area, dry toilets, rubbish disposal, a woodshed and *slask* (kitchen waste water) disposal. A separate cabin is normally provided for those walking with dogs and if not, a section of a cabin will be set aside exclusively for this purpose. All *stugor* are equipped with a *hjälptelefon* (emergency telephone) located in a small unlocked bunk room (*säkerhetsrum*) accessible all year round. Communal areas are clean, comfortable, warm and spacious, facilitating cooking (on the gas cookers provided), eating and socialising. Personal cleaning is generally restricted to cold water and soap outdoors. *Stugor* do not have electricity or Wi-Fi.

Outdoor shoes are not permitted inside cabins and all guests, campers and those staying indoors alike, are expected to assist with the domestic chores such as keeping communal areas clean, water collection, firewood sawing and chopping and *slask* disposal. Most, although not all, *stugor* have a drying room, a shop and a *bastu* (sauna). Some have a cabin dedicated to campers (*tältservicestuga*) consisting of a cooking and dining area. Most *stugor* now accept bank cards and those that don't are identified in the text.

Each shop (*butik*) at a *stuga* is classified as large, medium or small. All will sell some brand of trekking food and stove fuel, normally meths and gas; white gas is less common. Biscuits, snacks, soft drinks, tea, coffee, milk powder, batteries (AA and AAA normally), beer and some conventional foods will also be sold. Hoppers dispense dried foods such as muesli, rice, pasta and bran. Sugar sold at *stugor* comes only in single portion sachets, making it somewhat inconvenient to buy in bulk. The prices in *stuga* shops can be eye-watering and if you are saving weight

by buying exclusively at them the costs will soon rack up.

Stugor can be used on a day visitor basis by STF members and non-members alike; members for free, non-members for a small fee of SEK50. This allows access between 1100 and 1500 although this is rarely, if ever, strictly enforced.

THE TRUTH ABOUT SAUNA

Bastur are lit in the evenings and have hours that vary slightly from *stuga* to *stuga*. The most common timings are 1700–1830 for women, 1830–2000 for men, while 2000–2130 is mixed. The *bastur* are wood fired and have a water tank encircling the flue which provides hot water for washing. *Bastu* is often taken naked, although many choose to retain some clothing, be it shorts, pants or bra. The procedure is to enter and strip off in the entrance room. In the middle room there are bowls which can be filled with hot water from the flue tank and it is expected that all will wash themselves clean here before entering the inner room for some serious heat! The *bastu* is informal and a place where people go to wash, unwind and chat. It is not uncommon to enjoy a beer while sat in the *bastu*! When the heat grows intolerable, you dash out and dive into the lake to cool off. Shivering now after the plunge, you quickly return to the *bastu* inner for a second session. The inner is finally exited for a final wash in the middle room before

Fjällstuga bastu

dressing and departing; invigorated, clean and fresh. The *bastu* is one of the greatest joys of the Kungsleden and is highly recommended. It allows a high standard of personal hygiene to be maintained, muscles to be relaxed and social boundaries to be broken. If you are camping off site, you can use the *bastu* for SEK50.

TRAIL MARKING AND ACCESS

The Kungsleden is very easy to follow and is well-defined throughout. The summer route is marked by red paint on rocks and trees. The exception to this is Section 5 and the final two stages of Section 1, where in place of red paint, upright rocks and wooden posts are used to good effect.

Path junctions and key points are provided with clear signposts that indicate direction and distance information, not only to the next *fjällstuga* but also the one after. This is particularly useful if you're feeling strong and debating whether to push on further than you'd initially planned. The distances on these signposts are approximations and can be as much as 1–2km out. Winter trail markers will also be encountered (but not always followed) consisting of a red cross on a pole and very similar in appearance to British railway crossing markers. Raised wooden walkways are very common on the trail and these serve to mark the way as well as keep feet dry.

Allemansrätten allows everyone the right to enjoy Sweden's outdoors.

41

Summer and winter trail markers

It allows the public to roam freely, even on private land, to camp overnight and to pick mushrooms and berries. It also permits open fires to be lit although care must be taken during dry periods to prevent their spread; at all times only deadfall wood should be burnt. The right also brings the responsibility to treat plants and animals and other people's property with care. It can be summed up in the phrase 'don't disturb, don't destroy'. *Allemansrätten* is written into the Swedish constitution but it is not a law as such, rather a custom or part of the cultural heritage that has evolved and become accepted over the years.

WHAT TO TAKE

It is all too easy to carry too much weight, so take only what you will need – minimising your load will enhance your walking experience. You should be prepared for cold and wet conditions. This equates to good quality waterproofs, hat, gloves and warm layers. A broken-in pair of walking boots will also be essential, as will bespoke walking socks. A lightweight pair of camp shoes such as Crocs or flip-flops will allow you to air your feet at the day's end and ford swollen streams (you should not cross streams without shoes). Another option for crossing swollen streams are waterproof socks such as Sealskinz. These can be invaluable and save much time switching and then refitting footwear.

Be prepared for strong sun by carrying a set of light clothing (t-shirt and shorts), sun cream, sunglasses and a sun hat; for insects by carrying repellent, clothing that covers exposed skin and a head net. If pre-treating clothing against insects, ensure that only products specifically designed for fabrics are used.

With a few minor exceptions, water is plentiful on the trail. Carry a fold-out cup for drinking direct and a water bottle for the times when water is more scarce. Section 5 has reported issues with drinking water and carrying some form of water treatment would be sensible for this section.

It is always good practice to carry an emergency ration, whistle, small first aid kit and a head torch;

fjällstugor do not have electricity and a torch will be useful even when 24-hour daylight prevails. A map will allow a broader perspective and these can be acquired as needed and carried one at a time. Those intending to camp (wild or at the *stugor*) will require a tent, sleeping bag, roll mat, stove, fuel and food.

Those not carrying a tent and sleeping in the *stugor* will require a sleeping liner. They will also require a stove, fuel, food, sleeping bag and roll mat if they intend continuing onto Sections 3 and 4; a tent will not be necessary if the long days are walked as described in the accommodation section of this introduction. These items, if you didn't want to carry them the entire length of the Kungsleden, could be parcelled out, used and then returned at Kvikkjokk Fjällstation and Ammarnäs Livs depending on the direction of travel.

Swedish Krona (SEK), a small pack towel and basic toiletries are essential for anyone staying at the *stugor* or making use of the *bastu*. A mobile phone is useful for making some of the boat crossing arrangements in advance and researching at section ends when Wi-Fi and signal is available. Sweden is near to being a cashless society and a credit/debit card is essential for all walkers. Cash should also be carried in remoter areas, for paying boatmen and in case of power failures at electronic terminals.

Anything else is going to be optional and down to personal preference; walking poles, camera, reading book, battery pack, solar charger, chess set, seven pairs of underwear and so on; do you really need them?

The Naturum/tourist information and Ammarnäs Garden are co-located in central Ammarnäs (Stage 22)

MAPPING AND GPS

Section and stage maps are provided in this guidebook and are intended for planning purposes. There is no substitute for printed maps with regards to accuracy and clarity. A number of choices exist for such maps and given the Kungsleden's 460km length, they add surprisingly little bulk or weight to the walker's load.

Two map series are available at 1:100,000 scale, both printed on waterproof paper. The Lantmäteriet Sverige (Swedish Land Survey) Fjällkartan series covers the Kungsleden in six sheets and is printed on Pretex paper which while being waterproof, is not tear-resistant nor particularly robust. These are the only maps to provide magnetic variation information. The mapping takes up one side of the sheet while useful information (access rights, national parks, nature reserves, mountain safety, weather and GPS co-ordinates for emergency telephones) is provided on the reverse:

- BD6 Abisko-Kebnekaise-Narvik
  ISBN 978–91–588–9503–4
- BD8 Kebnekaise-Saltoluokta
  ISBN 978–91–588–9546–1
- BD10 Sarek National Park
  ISBN 978–91–588–9548–5
- BD14 Kvikkovik-Jäkkvik
  ISBN 978–91–588–9578–2
- BD16 Vouggatjålme-Ammarnäs
  ISBN 978–91–588–9580–5
- AC2 Tårnaby-Hemavan-Ammarnäs
  ISBN 978–91–588–9576–8

This series went out of print in July 2018 although should still be available via outlets for some time after. The mapping is now

Evening sun at Räverholmen (Stage 1a9)

available free for downloading or printing (at 1:50,000 and 1:10,000 scales) at www.lantmateriet.se/en/maps-and-geographic-information/Kartor/Papperskartor.

Four of Calazo's Fjällkartor map series cover the entire trail. These, also at 1:100,000 scale, are printed on tough and waterproof Tyvek paper:

- Calazo Fjällkartor Kebnekaisefjällen
  ISBN 978–91–867–7300–7
- Calazo Fjällkartor Sarek and Padjelanta
  ISBN 978–91–867–7301–4
- Calazo Fjällkartor Kvikkjokk, Ammarnäs and Arjeplog
  ISBN 978–91–883–3525–8
- Calazo Fjällkartor Vindelfjällen
  ISBN 978–91–883–3526–5

Norstedts produces the excellent Outdoorkartan 1:75,000 mapping series that is printed on Polyart, a synthetic paper which is completely waterproof and tear resistant. Mapping takes up both sides of the sheet with minimal space devoted to additional information. Again, six sheets cover the entire Kungsleden:

- Blad 1 Abisko-Kebenkaise-Nikkaluokta
  ISBN 978–91–1-306813–8
- Blad 2 Nikkaluokta-Sarek-Saltoluokta
  ISBN 978–91–1-306814–5
- Blad 3 Saltoluokta-Padjelanta-Kvikkovik
  ISBN 978–91–1-306815–2
- Blad 4 Kvikkovik-Jäkkvik
  ISBN 978–91–1-306816–9

- Blad 5 Jäkkvik-Ammarnäs
  ISBN 978–91–1-306817–6
- Blad 6 Ammarnäs-Hemavan-Lill-Björkvattnet
  ISBN 978–91–1-306818–3

Those undertaking the Abisko-Nikkaluokta circuit also have the option of 1:50:000 mapping in the guise of the Calazo 'Kebnekaise, Abisko och Riksgränsen' sheet (ISBN 978–91–88335–30–2).

Lantmäteriet Sverige provides excellent and free online mapping resources that walkers will find useful for planning http://kso.etjanster.lantmateriet.se/?lang=en. Sweden Topo Maps has a very good GPS-enabled app which includes 1:50,000 Fjällkartan mapping and a caching facility that allows the maps to be used offline. Functionality is comprehensive and includes the option to add waypoints, tracks and routes as you go; routes can be imported into the app for later navigation out on the ground. Many of the better functions (caching, importing routes) are only available in the Pro Version costing €6 for a year's subscription. Those thinking of using the app on the Kungsleden are advised to practise and trial it at home beforehand.

GPX tracks for the Kungsleden and Additional itineraries described in this guidebook can be downloaded free at www.cicerone.co.uk/982/GPX.

To function correctly, handheld GPS units must be set to the correct time zone, datum and position format. The grid system in use in Sweden is

SWEREF99TM which replaced RT90 in 2007. Old GPS units will have RT90 installed as a datum while new units will have SWEREF99TM. All paper maps use the new SWEREF99TM co-ordinate system, although the Lantmäteriet Sverige series still has the old RT90 co-ordinate marks around the margins and is therefore still compatible with older GPS units.

The convention in Sweden is to give grid references with the northing first and the easting second. Therefore, if providing grid references in an emergency, it would be best to use the prefixes north and east prior to giving the numerals.

COMMUNICATIONS AND ELECTRONICS

Charging batteries

Many modern devices only have the option to recharge an internal battery (mobile phones, iPods, fitness trackers and even head torches) or to charge a rechargeable battery (cameras). Nearly everyone will have need for recharging while walking the Kungsleden where there is no access to mains electricity save at the section ends. Even here power sockets will be at a premium in communal areas and dorms. Booking a private room is the only way to guarantee unfettered access to charging at the section ends. Sweden uses the Europlug (Type C & F) with two round prongs; the mains electric voltage is 220 volts.

It is possible to charge on the trail and not be reliant on the scant availability of mains electricity. A simple option is to carry a pre-charged high-capacity battery pack. These can be quite heavy, but will guarantee power.

Another option is to carry a solar charger, of which there are a bewildering number of makes and models. There are some guiding principles when it comes to choosing a solar charger. Firstly, avoid buying small and/or cheap; it may seem like a pocket-sized bargain, but it will let you down either by being feeble or not working at all. Choose a charger that can be easily and robustly mounted on your rucksack so it can charge all day. Some units provide only direct charge, while others charge an internal battery for later use, and some do both. The ability to do both maximises your generating opportunities. All solar chargers perform best in strong sunlight, but try to choose one that also has good low-light performance, there will be days on the Kungsleden when that is all you will get. Even good-brand solar chargers can have poor soldering. Try to choose a charger that is uncomplicated (fewer solders) and has a reputation for being robust. Although not comprehensive, www.outdoorgearlab.com is a good place to start your research into solar chargers, or any other outdoor equipment for that matter.

When it comes to charging on the go, try not to be wholly reliant on one mode of charging. And be sensible

– being smart and prepared when it comes to recharging is all well and good, keeping devices switched on when not in use is not!

Phones

Apart from the section ends, the vast majority of the Kungsleden is devoid of mobile phone coverage. There are times however when a mobile phone is useful, the most obvious example being for arranging boat crossings. These occasions are indicated in the text, as are the points on the ground where a signal is available; the network with the best coverage would seem to be the Telia network. If using a phone for GPS navigation, ensure the mapping is cached before leaving home. With mobile signal being scant your mobile phone cannot be viewed or relied upon as any use in an emergency.

The international dialling code for Sweden is +46. Should you be lucky enough to have a signal when you require assistance the emergency services number is 112. The non-emergency number for the police (*polis*) and other assistance in Sweden is 11414.

RESUPPLY

Some thought will be required about sustaining your walk on the Kungsleden and fortunately you have a number of options. How you go about it will be decided by three factors: cost, how much of the trail you intend walking, and how much weight you want to carry. Most walkers bring food for the first section with

The shop at Teusajaure Fjällstuga is classed as 'large' by the STF (Stage 7)

them from home, what happens after that will require planning.

Shops

Food and fuel supplies are readily available at the start of every section irrespective of the direction of travel. Abisko, Saltoluotka and Kvikkjokk have shops in the *fjällstationer*. Abisko, Hemavan, Jäkkvik and Ammarnäs all have supermarkets, although dehydrated trekking food can't be guaranteed at these outlets. The cost in the *fjällstationer* will be expensive; in the supermarkets, less so.

Sections 1, 2 and 5 allow you the choice of purchasing in the *fjällstuga* shops as you go and you will need to carry no more than two days of food at a time. This will minimise rucksack weight – but at the cost of higher prices.

Delivery services

Another option is to pre-purchase food, parcel it out and collect it as you pass through. This is possible for every section; Saltoluotka and Kvikkjokk *fjällstationer* offer parcel holding for a small fee, while in Jäkkvik and Ammarnäs, the Handlar'n and Livs supermarkets respectively are Bussgods agents www.bussgods. se (Swedish only). Bussgods is an internal Swedish distribution service that uses the long-distance bus network to make deliveries and so is able to offer keen prices. The drawback with Bussgods for overseas visitors is that your parcel has to be fed into

the system via a Bussgods agent from within Sweden. Such an approach only works therefore if you have time in the country before beginning the trail to shop, pack and dispatch. Contact information for the Handlar'n and Livs supermarket is included in the text. The staff at both are extremely helpful and it may be possible to ship direct to them from overseas without having to use the Bussgods network.

Shipping parcels directly from overseas is expensive and will need careful evaluation as to whether the cost and effort are worth the saving made over purchasing in Sweden. There will be a saving to be made against purchasing in the *fjällstationer* and *fjällstugor*, less so where the supermarkets are concerned.

Whatever the mode of shipping, Bussgods or direct, it is always best to contact the receiver by email beforehand. This will allow you to confirm their holding charges and how long they will hold your parcel for; generally two weeks, although longer if negotiated beforehand. If, for whatever reason, your parcel doesn't arrive, there is always the reassurance that you can purchase at the *fjällstation* or the supermarket in question.

SAFETY AND WELLBEING

Medical facilities and insurance

Sweden has excellent medical facilities and visitors from other EU countries are entitled to reciprocal rights if they carry an EHIC (European Health Insurance Card) with them; it has yet to be confirmed whether UK citizens will continue to enjoy EHIC-type rights and benefits post-Brexit. Cards are only available from your country of residence and must be obtained prior to travel. A multi-lingual EHIC phone app is available which explains how to use the EHIC card and summarises treatments, costs, procedures for reimbursement and emergency numbers for all EU countries including Sweden. For non-emergency health advice you should ring 1177. Medical facilities are limited on and near to the Kungsleden due to the remote nature of the region. Those on medication or prescriptions should bring sufficient for the duration of their trek. A small basic first aid kit

will allow you to deal with minor day-to-day issues.

EHIC card or not, all walkers are advised to obtain comprehensive insurance that covers for injury, illness, emergency rescue, medical fees, air ambulance and repatriation. When arranging cover it is important that the policy covers for all eventualities you might meet and does not have significant exclusions. The key exclusions to check for are HELICASEVAC and rescue and also for specified activities such as 'remote trekking' and geographical definitions such as 'Arctic areas' and 'Arctic Circle'.

Water

Water on the Kungsleden is generally regarded as safe to drink. The exception is on Section 5 where walkers have reported illness suspected of being water related. Walkers are advised to treat drinking water on this section by boiling, using a simple treatment such as chlorine tablets or using a lightweight filter such as the Sawyer Mini Water Filtration System.

Pests

Arctic summers experience high numbers of insects and the Kungsleden is no exception. The spring thaw produces large areas of standing and stagnant water, ideal conditions for insect larvae such as the mosquito (*mygga*) to hatch. The first strong frosts in mid to late August kill off most insects but, until that time, you will need to travel prepared. Long-sleeved clothing and trousers will protect your limbs, light gloves your hands. A wide-brimmed hat with an integral net that hangs free of your face will offer far better protection than just a simple head net. Carry and use a good insect repellent of which there are very many available. Maybe surprisingly, Avon Skin So Soft moisturiser is a very effective insect repellent, and has the added advantage of being kind on fabrics and plastics. Many proprietary insect repellents are not so kind. If camping, avoid pitching beside standing water and dense foliage; if feasible, choose a spot that catches the breeze slightly. Biting insects are at their worst when the air is still, and also in the evenings once the sun has set.

Large animals

Sweden has a number of indigenous species that are potentially dangerous; the brown bear, wolverine and the moose. All these are very wary of humans and will keep well away, avoiding contact if given the opportunity; walkers should consider themselves lucky to catch a glimpse of any of the three. If you do, do not get too close, do not take them unawares and do not go anywhere near a bear with cubs. If charged by a bear try to appear large and make as much aggressive noise as you are able, to scare and bluff the bear. If you are attacked, curl up into a ball and use your arms to protect your head.

Emergencies

The number for the emergency services in Sweden is 112. Unless you are lucky to be in an area with mobile reception or are close to an emergency shelter equipped with an emergency telephone, you will be reliant on the kindness and assistance of others in an emergency. If someone else has to go for help then you may be waiting many hours for evacuation and treatment, a period you may have to survive by your wits. There are no police stations or staff at any of the six access points to the Kungsleden and therefore non-emergency police support should be sought via 11414, the nearest police stations are all at least an hour's drive east of the Kungsleden at Kiruna, Gällivare, Jokkmokk, Arjeplog and Tärnaby.

USING THIS GUIDE

The trail is described from north to south, and divided into five sections bounded by transport access points. Each of the five sections can be viewed as an independent entity and walked as such. The sections are composed of 28 stages of varying length, determined principally by the availability of accommodation; this is especially the case for Sections 1, 2 and 5. Some of the stages are very short and may be combined if so desired. If walking without a tent you will be restricted to the accommodation available at stage ends;

self-contained walkers with tents are at liberty to divide the trail up as they please.

Sections are individually introduced and accompanied by a 1:400,000 overview map; access information is also provided. Each stage then includes a more detailed 1:100,000 map, and a route profile to illustrate the ups and downs. Each stage begins with a summary of the route in terms of distance, approximate time required, ascent, descent, and so on.

Distances have been measured using GPS, while ascent and descent have been measured with a digital barometric altimeter. Distances and timings provided are for walking only and additional time will need to be factored in for rests and boat crossings depending on whether they are rowed or motorised (see individual stage descriptions and Appendix C for guidance on water crossing timings).

Walking times are provided with the caveat that everyone covers the ground at a different speed. Timings can only ever be at best a guide and not an absolute. It should soon become apparent whether you are moving slower or faster and by how much, which will then allow for a personal extrapolation of timings. Timings provided are consistent throughout for a non-hurried self-contained walker carrying camping equipment and food. Timings do not make allowances for rests, stops or any other such halt on the trail.

Each stage has a difficulty grading based upon three criteria; the stage length, the amount of ascent, and the going underfoot:

- **Easy:** short, little ascent and good underfoot
- **Moderate:** one or two criteria being unfavourable
- **Challenging:** all three criteria being unfavourable

As for timings, the grading should not be regarded as an absolute, but as a measure against which other stages can be compared.

Good camp spots are identified in the text and on the stage maps, and although not exhaustive, should allow those camping to identify poor areas and make timely decisions as to whether or not to push on for the day. In extremis it is always possible to make camp somewhere, however, the purpose of identifying sites is to enhance the camping experience. Camped through-hiking of the Kungsleden is popular and such information has been included in the main to benefit this community.

Prior liaison and arrangement will avoid delay at some of the motorised water crossings. Therefore, a prompt to action is included at an appropriately early point in a preceding stage to that in which the crossing occurs; this is also provided for those walking northwards.

Throughout the route description directions 'left' and 'right' refer to the direction of travel only, points of the compass are used for all other directions. Where used to describe bus services or opening hours, 'daily' indicates Monday to Sunday inclusive. Some Swedish and Sámi terms have been retained and used in this guidebook due to the universality of their use or the lack of a good English equivalent. Examples include *bastu*, *fjällstuga*, *fjällstation*, *kåta* and *servishus* (utilities building).

All costs quoted are as of spring 2019 (exchange rate £1 = SEK11.55 = €1.13) and may be subject to inflation and change.

Leaving Servestugan (Stage 25)

SECTION 1 – ABISKO TO SALTOLUOKTA

Traversing the Tjäktjavagge en route to Sälka (Stage 4)

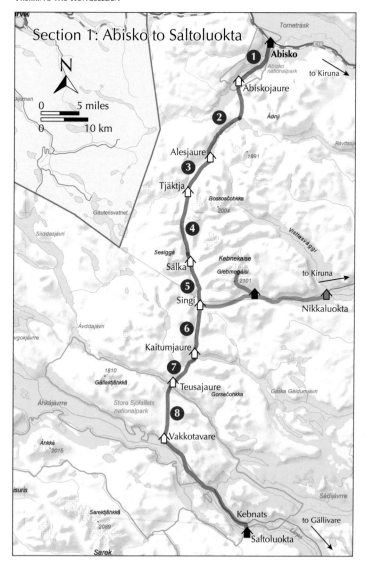

Section 1: Abisko to Saltoluokta

N

0   5 miles

0   10 km

Torneträsk

① Abisko
Abisko
nationalpark
to Kiruna

② Abiskojaure

Ádnji

Alesjaure
③
1991

Tjäktja
Bossosčohkka
2004

④

Sealggá
Sälka
Kebnekaise
Giebmegáisi
2101

⑤
Singi
to Kiruna

Nikkaluokta

⑥
Kaitumjaure

⑦
Teusajaure
Gorsačohkka
Gáška Gáidumjávri

1810
Gállaktjåhkkå

Åhkåjávrre
Stora Sjöfallets
nationalpark

⑧
Vakkotavare

Åhkká
2015

Sarektjåhkkå
2089

Kebnats
to Gällivare

Saltoluokta

Sarek

SECTION 1
Abisko to Saltoluokta

Start	Abisko
Finish	Vakkotavare (bus link to Saltoluokta to continue the Kungsleden)
Distance	108.8km to Vakkotavare; 136km to Saltoluokta (walking distance 105.3km)
Ascent	1645m
Descent	1560m
Terrain	Mountain and fell, minimal forest
High point	Tjäktja Pass 1150m (Stage 4)
Boat crossings	Mandatory: Teusajaure and Langas (3.5km); optional: Alisjávri
Note	30.7km of water crossing and bus journey

This first and northernmost section of the Kungsleden is the most celebrated and busy of all the five sections. It is also the least forested section, being overwhelmingly open fell and mountain in character. There are a number of reasons for the section's popularity, including the good transport links serving the section ends. While the terrain is the most beautifully stark and remote on the entire Kungsleden, this is mitigated by good trail marking and a regular network of STF *fjällstugor*. These allow the barren landscape to be safely covered with minimal experience, weight and equipment.

The section begins gently in birch forest before climbing onto the high open fells beyond Abiskojaure. The landscape becomes more rugged and mountainous as the Tjäktja Pass is approached. This, the highest point on the Kungsleden, is rarely entirely free of snow even in midsummer. South of the Tjäktja the impressive 30km Tjäktjavagge glacial valley is transited in its entirety. South of the Tjäktjavagge the landscape softens and the views expand to include the wonderful mountains of Sarek to the southwest. The section concludes with a couple of stages that leapfrog from lakeside to lakeside via magnificent open fell plateaus. At Vakkotavare there is the option to depart the Kungsleden or catch a bus that will link into the second section, starting from Saltoluokta.

Additional itineraries

Many walkers follow the Kungsleden southwards as far as Singi (end of Stage 5) before turning eastward towards Kebnekaise to complete the Abisko-Nikkaluokta Circuit (see Additional itinerary 1); a comfortable week's walking through some of the Kungsleden's very best scenery. With Kiruna as the point of access transport links in and out are straightforward and the route is well equipped with STF services for those who desire them. For those seeking a measure of solitude, quiet spots for wild camping are easily found.

For those walking Additional itinerary 1 between Singi and Nikkaluokta, an ascent of Kebnekaise, Sweden's highest peak, is an opportunity well worth considering. Although it makes for a long day, the return trip to the summit (see Additional itinerary 2) is immensely satisfying. In clear weather the views are sublimely unending and the sense of achievement is likely to crown your trip. The non-technical Västra Leden (West Route) is very well marked throughout and no less than three emergency shelters high on the mountain provide security in marginal weather. Guiding services are available at Kebnekaise STF Fjällstation.

Access

Abisko is served by direct SJ trains from Stockholm (17hr) which includes excellent overnight sleeper services. Flying to Kiruna from Stockholm (1hr 30min) is another good option followed by an onward bus (1hr 30min) or train (1hr-plus) to Abisko.

The trail can be exited at Vakkotavare by the 93 bus to Gällivare and from there onward by SJ train or flight to Stockholm.

Maps

- 1:75,000 Outdoorkartan Blad 1 (Abisko-Kebnekaise-Nikkaluokta) and Blad 2 (Nikkaluokta-Sarek-Saltoluokta) OR
- 1:100,000 Fjällkartan BD6 (Abisko-Kebnekaise-Narvik) and BD8 (Kebnekaise-Saltoluokta) OR
- 1:100,000 Calazo Fjällkartor Kebnekaisefjällen.
- 1:50,000 Calazo (Kebnekaise, Abisko och Riksgränsen) covers Stages 1–5.

If walking Additional itinerary 1, you will only need a single map: 1:75,000 Outdoorkartan Blad 1 (Abisko-Kebnekaise-Nikkaluokta), 1:100,000 Fjällkartan BD6 (Abisko-Kebnekaise-Narvik), 1:100,000 Calazo Fjällkartor Kebnekaisefjällen or 1:50,000 Calazo (Kebnekaise, Abisko och Riksgränsen).

For Additional itinerary 2 (Kebnekaise summit), Calazo 1:15,000 Hög Alpin Karta Kebnekaise is recommended.

Kiruna

The town is dominated by the massive LKAB iron-ore mine and consequently it has an industrial air about it. ▶ Due to mining subsidence, a long-term relocation project is under way in Kiruna which will see the town centre move about 2km to the east of its current location. Some of the older historic buildings such as the church will be moved to new sites. Once complete, the intent is to mine on the site of the current town centre.

If flying into Kiruna, a bus links the airport to the bus station in the centre of town from where the 91 and Hörvalls Nikkaluoktaexpressen bus services can be caught for Abisko (1hr 30min) and Nikkaluokta (1hr 15min) respectively. From the bus station a free service takes passengers to the SJ railway station which is on the edge of town. Journey time is 10min. The town has a number of accommodation options that include the Yellow House Hostel (www.yellowhouse.nu – Swedish only), excellent camping at Ripan (www.ripan.se/en) and a number of hotels. A small Co-op (10mins from town centre) sells conventional foods but

The LKAB mine is the largest and most modern underground iron-ore mine in the world.

Kiruna will be the last opportunity to use an ATM before commencing the trail.

no dehydrated brands for trekking. Intersport is open daily and offers gas, meths and white gas as well as maps, basic outdoor equipment and Adventure Food dehydrated meals. The excellent and comprehensively stocked Vildmarkshörnan (www.vildsmarkshornan.com – Swedish only) will have anything you might need in terms of equipment for the trail. ◂

Abisko

This small town is a local tourist hub for walkers, fishermen and naturalists. Most services and facilities are to be found in eastern Abisko close to Abisko Östra railway station. The Godisfabriken supermarket and petrol station does not sell trekking foods but is otherwise very well stocked. Meths (but no gas or white gas) can be sourced at the store which is open daily between 1000 and 2000; the Aurora snack-bar trailer is conveniently located just outside the store in season selling hot dogs, soups, burgers (reindeer, moose and beef) and meatballs. A range of accommodation options are available in Abisko including the centrally located Abisko Guesthouse (www.abiskoguesthouse.com) and the Abisko Fjällturer hostel (www.abisko.net). There is no ATM in Abisko.

Downtown Abisko

Kungsleden display at Abisko Fjällstation

ABISKO STF FJÄLLSTATION

Many arriving in Abisko will alight from the SJ train at Abisko Turistation and head for the *fjällstation* some 200m away. This is the northernmost *fjällstation* in Sweden, some 250km within the Arctic Circle. The facility is large and comprehensive, offering camping, four and six-bed self-catering cabins, an STF youth hostel and more than 100 hotel standard beds. The camping area is 250m east of the main building and is provided with a *servishus* comprising showers, toilets, wash-up area and rubbish bins; there are no cooking facilities for those camping. The main building offers all services; accommodation, *bastu*, restaurant, guided activities, Wi-Fi, bar and information boards (train and bus timetables, weather forecast). The very well-stocked shop sells the full range of Blå Band dehydrated trekking food, all fuel types, maps, nature guides, conventional foods and outdoor clothing and equipment; bank cards are accepted. It is well worth visiting the *fjällstation*'s new Naturum which has a book shop and provides travel information and detailed environmental information about the Abisko National Park.

STAGE 1
Abisko to Abiskojaure

Start	Abisko 385m
Finish	Abiskojaure STF Fjällstuga 490m
Distance	13.3km
Ascent	115m
Descent	10m
Grade	Easy
Time	4hr 50min
Terrain	Good trail and boardwalks throughout, some minor ascent. Boardwalks immediately north of the Nissonjokk campsite quickly become inundated following rain
Shelter	Open-sided shelter at Nissonjokk
Camping	Wild – only permitted on the official site at Nissonjokk. Paid – Abiskojaure STF Fjällstuga
Resupply	Shop at Abiskojaure STF Fjällstuga

This relatively short and undemanding first stage is confined to the Abisko National Park, a 77km^2 area of mountain valley that was established in 1909 and since 1966, has formed part of the larger Torneträsk Biosphere Reserve. The stage is ideal for shaking out, stretching the legs and getting accustomed to the pack. The close proximity of Abisko Turistation to the trail's start means that it is possible, for those that are prepared, to step off the train and begin walking immediately. Many day walkers will be seen on this stage and it is a popular activity to stay in the *fjällstuga* at Abiskojaure overnight, before returning to Abisko the following day. The views are initially confined by the birch forest as the trail closely parallels the Abiskojåkka River. The second half of the stage has a more open aspect alongside Abiskojaure Lake where dwarf tree species start to become more prevalent and mountain vistas begin to open up. Camping options within the park are limited to the official site at Nissonjokk.

The trail's start is well signposted and clearly identified by a dedicated wooden gateway which is located 100m south of the E10 and within 5min walk of both the

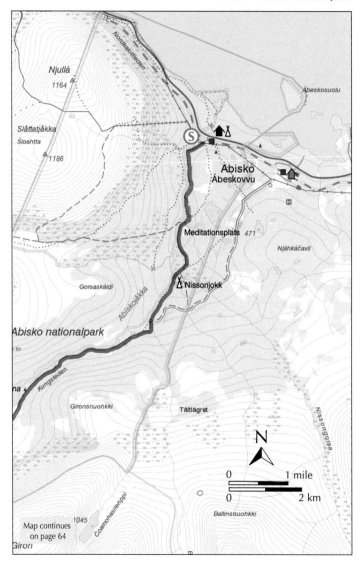

Map continues
on page 64

The gateway provides information about Abisko National Park, its regulations, and the meditation trail that will be encountered along the way.

fjällstation and Abisko Turistation. ◄ From the gateway, follow the wide trail southwards through birch forest, accompanied by the sound of the noisy **Abiskojåkka River**. Although a variety of local trail markers will be seen attached to the trees, follow the red paint markers from the outset. Small glimpses of peaks will be snatched through the birch, but it is not until 1.5km, at a rise over an old dolomite quarry, that the first proper views are to be had. Atop the rise and in a perfect setting overlooking a bend in the river you will find the first of seven *meditationsplatser* (**meditation spots**) that are located along the Dag Hammarskjöld Way between Abisko and Nikkaluokta.

> **Dag Hammarskjöld** (1905–1961) was an accomplished Swedish diplomat who went on to serve as the second UN Secretary General from 1953 to 1961. Killed in an air crash while on a peace mission to the Congo, he is the only Nobel Peace Prize Laureate to have received the award posthumously.

Descend from the quarry and follow long sections of boardwalk provided for negotiating the more boggy

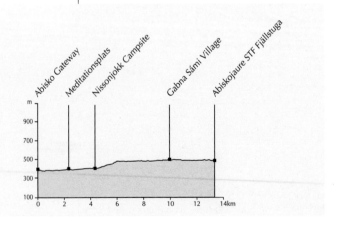

areas. After 1.5km, cross a metal suspension bridge span-
ning the Nissonjohka River. The Nissonjohka is a tributary of the Abiskojåkka and here, just before joining the
larger river, it flows as a series of braided streams, the
bridge crossing the largest of the channels. Once across
the bridge, follow the boardwalks which here are provided to negotiate the smaller channels and reach the
official campsite, **Nissonjokk**, a few minutes after crossing the bridge.

The Abiskojåkka

> Nissonjokk campsite – in addition to an area for
> tents, this campsite has dry latrines and an open-
> sided shelter fitted with seating and a wood burner.
> (Latrines on the trail are enclosed in a small wooden
> hut and come furnished with a seat.) Campfire pits
> and rubbish disposal are also provided.

Continue close to the Abiskojåkka and after 2km,
take a second bridge across another tributary, the
Ballinjohka; be sure to turn left off the bridge and then

63

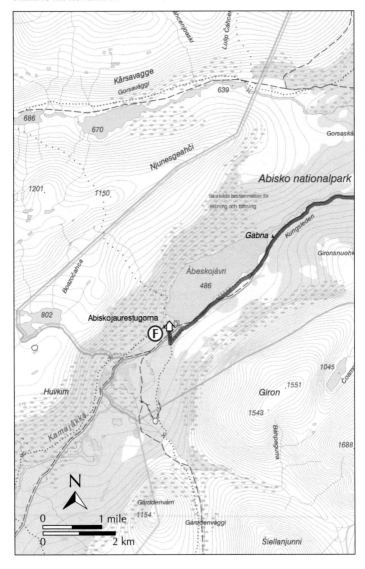

immediately right to keep on course. ▶ Once across the Ballinjohka, the birch trees become sparser and smaller giving the overall impression of a more expansive landscape. In places there are multiple boardwalks, a single line for walkers and twin lines to accommodate the all-terrain vehicles (ATVs) which are popular and heavily utilised by the Sámi when travelling to and from their summer settlements. Pass a latrine just before reaching the northeastern extreme of **Ábeskojávri Lake**. A little further on besides the lakeshore itself, lies the small Sámi village of **Gabna**, a fascinating mix of traditional *kåtor* and modern wooden builds. From the village continue easily along the eastern shore of the lake, which is overlooked by the dark steep face of Giron (1551m) to the east. At the lake's southwestern end, follow signs for Abiskojaure and 'Unna Allakas 24' and cross the metal suspension bridge over the wide **Kamajåkka River** to reach the lakeside site of Abiskojaure STF Fjällstuga (**Abiskojaurestugorna**).

It is possible to reach this point directly from Abisko Östra railway station although it would involve fording the Nissonjohka River en route.

Crossing the Kamajåkka River

ABISKOJAURE STF FJÄLLSTUGA (490M)

Wheelchair access at the fjällstuga

Abiskojaure is one of the STF's oldest *fjällstugor* and although plans existed as early as 1903, it wasn't until 1907 that the STF was able to establish a presence on the site following the gift of a cabin by a local power company; a second cabin was added by the STF in 1911. The *fjällstuga* has beds for 61 spread across a loose circle of cabins. Campers and day visitors benefit from a dedicated *tältservicestuga* equipped with tables and chairs, gas cookers and utensils. The tent pitches are among the nearby trees behind the woodshed although care should be taken not to pitch too close to the nearby helipad! The entire site is furnished with raised boardwalks and ramps to allow wheelchair access, the first *fjällstuga* to be so equipped and a gift from the STF to the Swedish king, Carl XVI Gustaf. The shop is well-stocked and accepts bank cards as well as cash. The *fjällstuga* has a *bastu* and although not posted, a weather forecast is available on request from the *stugvärdar*. Details are posted for the optional motorised crossing that will be encountered on Stage 2.

STAGE 2
Abiskojaure to Alesjaure

Start	Abiskojaure STF Fjällstuga 490m
Finish	Alesjaure STF Fjällstuga 780m
Distance	20.3km
Ascent	345m
Descent	55m
Grade	Moderate
Time	6hr 50min
Terrain	Thinning birch forest then open fell. Good trail throughout, although rocky in places
Shelter	Open-sided shelter at the wooden boat jetty
Camping	Wild – once out of the Abisko National Park wild camping is permitted anywhere. Room for many tents 50m prior to the bridge across the Sielajohka River. Many other small spots once south of Gárddenvággi although care will be required to find a wholly dry site. Good sites immediately south of and across the bridge from Alesjaure STF Fjällstuga. Paid – Alesjaure STF Fjällstuga
Resupply	Shop at Alesjaure STF Fjällstuga

The second day trades the immediacy of the trail start for the remoteness of the mountains and some will find it a long and tiring walk following the easy introduction of the initial stage. Although relatively drawn out and moderately steep to start, the ascent through Gárddenvággi is gradual and rewards the walker with expansive views across a lake-strewn valley to the imposing wall of the Kåtotjåkka Massif beyond. Those that choose to make use of the seasonal motorised service across Alisjávri will cut the final (although easiest) 5km off their day's walk.

Retrace the trail out from Abiskojaure, back across the **Kamajåkka** and then follow the path southwards as it climbs gently uphill through thinning birch forest. ▶ Two kilometres from Abiskojaure a notice board marks the boundary and your departure from the Abisko National Park, from here onwards, wild camping is permitted anywhere.

Ahead, the view is dominated by the conical Gárddenvárri (1154m) which guards entry to Gárddenvággi.

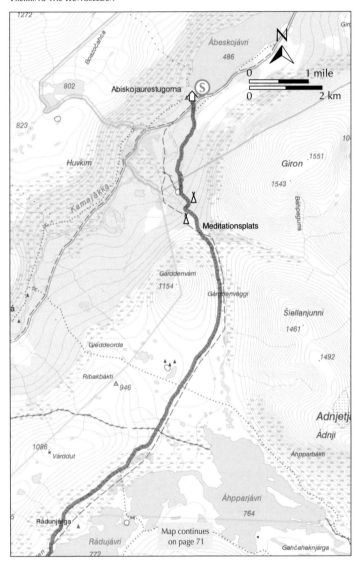

Map continues
on page 71

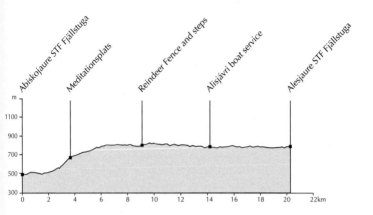

Follow the steepening trail and very soon the roar of the Šiellajohka River will be heard up ahead. A metal suspension bridge spans a gorge and 50m prior, a latrine and camp spots for many tents are passed among the trees. Cross the bridge to where the treeline is reached and continue more steeply over open ground as the trail begins its ascent into the **Gárddenvággi**. Within 20 minutes the **second meditationsplats** of the Dag Hammarskjöld Way will be passed and this is a good opportunity to pause, rest and take in the view back across to Abiskojaure. Continue climbing, less steeply now as the rocky and uneven path hugs the lower eastern slopes of **Gárddenvárri**. Ahead a shallow ridge will be seen descending from the west to intersect the path. The crest of the ridge marks the end of the day's main ascent and from here a Sámi village will be seen close by on the right. To the south, a magnificent vista of long lakes and mountains is revealed to spur you onwards. Continue level before ascending gently to a reindeer fence that is crossed by large wooden steps. A notice board at the fence has information detailing the Alisjávri boat service which is 5km further along the trail. ▶

Continue along the trail which undulates parallel to and elevated above the shores of first Miesákjávri and

The fence marks the reindeer grazing boundary between the Gabna and Leavas Sámi villages.

then **Rádujávri Lake**. Just over half way between the reindeer fence and the boat service a reindeer herder's cabin will be seen down towards Rádujávri. On reaching the rapids that mark the **outflow of Alisjávri** into Rádujávri, you will almost be upon the boat service which is overlooked from across the lake by the impressive black cliffs of Njuikkostakbákti (1370m).

At this, its north terminus, the Alisjávri boat service consists of an open-sided metal shelter, wooden jetty, flag pole and a latrine. When conditions are good, Alesjaure STF Fjällstuga can be seen 5km away to the south. In season, boats depart at 1030, 1530, 1730 and 1900. From Alesjaure, where the boat originates, departures are at 1000, 1500, 1700 and 1830. Those wishing to take the boat to Alesjaure should raise the yellow flag to indicate they are waiting as the operator cannot be wholly relied upon to come every time, especially when the weather is inclement or there are no passengers from Alesjaure. Prices are SEK350 each way, half price for children and unaccompanied bags. The service is operated by local Sámi and it is possible to be dropped off at Alisjávri

Heading southwards alongside Rádujávri

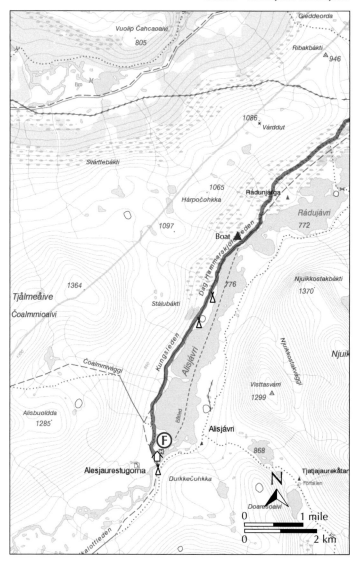

village from where, it is a 30min walk to the *fjällstuga* at Alesjaure.

If not taking the boat, continue on the trail which now runs close to the shoreline of **Alisjávri**. The path very soon becomes less rocky and the going the best of the day. Follow the trail for 2km passing two *rengärde* in short succession; across the lake to the south, the Sámi village of Alisjávri (also known as Leava) will be seen. ◄ Boots may have to be removed to cross the **Čoalmmivággi stream**, a far more likely prospect following heavy rainfall. Alesjaure STF Fjällstuga (**Alesjaurestugorna**) occupies an elevated position on a rocky bluff and should now be clearly visible ahead at the lake's end. Continue easily, crossing sandy beaches at times, for the last stretch to the *fjällstuga*.

Brush and heather are common and represent an ideal habitat for the wildfowl that can be seen along this stretch.

ALESJAURE STF FJÄLLSTUGA (780M)

The original STF *fjällstuga* was located some 3km to the southwest of its current location. Following a fire that destroyed one of the buildings during the 1977–78 season, it was decided to relocate the *fjällstuga* to its current location; the cause of the fire was suspected – although not proven – to be alcohol related. The decision to relocate was in part due to requests from the Sámi, whose reindeer grazing grounds the original *fjällstuga* had occupied.

The new *fjällstuga* was inaugurated in March 1985 and now consists of a large number of buildings. The facility belongs to the Swedish state and is leased by the STF. It was intended that the rebuilt facility would be used as a conference centre and thus, uniquely on the Kungsleden, the *stugvärd* area is equipped with tables and chairs for communal use. The entire site is elevated on a rocky bluff above the delta of the Aliseatnu River and is open and exposed to the weather.

Alesjaure has the highest number of bed spaces – 86 – of any STF *fjällstuga* in Sweden. The camp spots are average at best, being small and off the level. Camping is permitted anywhere in the vicinity of the *fjällstuga*, although the best spots are just off and to the south of the rocky bluff, above the Aliseatnu. Equally good if not better pitches can be found a short distance away on the far (eastern) bank where there is a simple bench and oil drum barbecue. These camp spots are free. Alesjaure has no dedicated

Alesjaure STF Fjällstuga viewed from the north

tältservicestuga although those paying to camp can use the facilities in any of the three overnight cabins. The shop is well-stocked with food (dehydrated trekking and conventional), fuel (gas and meths), batteries, maps and beer. Bank cards are accepted as well as cash. The *fjällstuga* also has a *bastu* and two rooms dedicated to those walking with dogs. Daily weather forecasts are available from the *stugvärdar*. Alesjaure is served by a daily helicopter flight in season which departs Abisko for Alesjaure at 0830 and departs Alesjaure for the return at 0850. Flights cost SEK1000 each way – more when arranged outside this schedule.

If you have the time and energy, Alisjávri village is a mere 30-min walk away. This substantial village consists of about 100 buildings.

STAGE 3
Alesjaure to Tjäktja

Start	Alesjaure STF Fjällstuga 780m
Finish	Tjäktja STF Fjällstuga 1015m
Distance	13.1km
Ascent	265m
Descent	30m
Grade	Moderate
Time	4hr 45min
Terrain	Open and exposed river valley with a final pull up into a stark mountain landscape. Boggy in places, although boardwalks are provided in the worst areas. Stream wading may be required during wet periods
Shelter	Nil
Camping	Wild – many opportunities for wild camping. Paid – Tjäktja STF Fjällstuga
Resupply	Nil

The trail along the wide Alisvággi is not demanding, so you can pause and reflect at will. Most of the effort is to be found in the final section, consisting of a broad stream fan that may require wading and a final steep pull up to the magnificently positioned *fjällstuga*. The landscape at Tjäktja is a barren contrast to that experienced thus far on the trail; do not be surprised to find snow patches near or on the path, even in midsummer. There are plenty of camp spots en route for those seeking solitude in nature. Despite the relatively short length of this stage, many depart Alesjaure early due to there being limited bed space available at Tjäktja, and continue to Sälka where there is more space and a shop.

This is prime wildfowl habitat and reindeer herding country so keep a lookout as you progress southwards.

Cross the **Aliseatnu** via the metal suspension bridge and continue along the trail southwards into the **Alisvággi**. The valley is flat and open affording good views ahead. The rounded hills that flank the valley will now seem more immediate and many will be flecked with snow fields all year round. ◄ On drawing level with the Unna

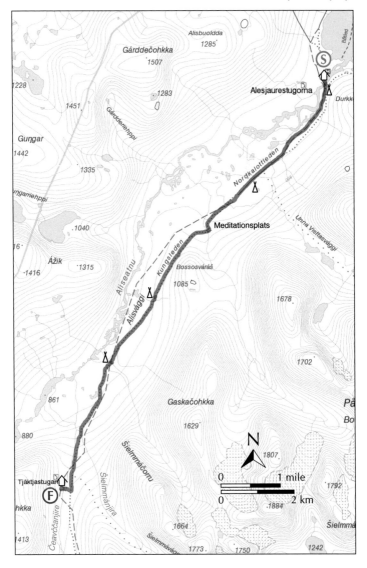

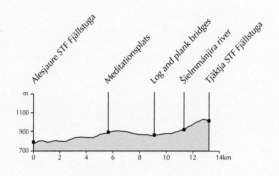

Visttasvággi, a good camp spot is passed, the first of many during the day's walk. A little further on, the southern outflow from the Unna Visttasvággi may require wading during wet weather.

Follow the trail gently uphill and very soon you reach the **third meditationsplats** of the Dag Hammarskjöld Way. As ever, these spots allow you to pause to think and soak up the views. Interestingly, all three *meditationsplatser* encountered thus far have been located close to a river. Cross the metal suspension bridge that spans the Bossosjohka River 200m further on. Continue the gentle climb from the bridge to a point where you reach a crest on the northwest flanks of **Bossosváraš** (1085m); the views both north and south open up here and this is your last opportunity to look back towards Alesjaure and the way you have come. This spot also represents the midpoint of the day's walking.

Descend past a good camp spot just right of the path. The site is somewhat open and exposed but is flat, level, dry and has space for a number of tents. This spot can be identified by a distinct and almost cubic-shaped rock that stands beside the trail.

Continue descending and cross two distinct log and plank bridges beyond which more camp spots will be found which as previously, are flat, level and dry, although slightly exposed. From here the trail begins its ascent towards Tjäktja and the dark steep face of Lulip Muorahisčohkka (1413m), beneath which the *fjällstuga* sits, can now be clearly seen. With your sights fixed on Tjäktja, follow the trail gently uphill and after 2km, negotiate the **Šielmmánjira River**. Although relatively shallow at this point, the river has fanned out to become 25m wide and great care is required if you are to reach the far side with dry feet. Those wearing waterproof socks can merely stride confidently across, those without will follow wobbling from stone to stone.

Having crossed the Šielmmánjira, continue more steeply now, accompanied by the rising roar of the **Čeavččanjire River** that thunders through the nearby gorge; Tjäktja STF Fjällstuga (**Tjäktjastugan**) will be clearly visible across on the other side. As the trail levels out, keep following it past the *fjällstuga* to a wooden sign that sends you right and across a metal suspension bridge. Once across, double back the final 200m to the fjällstuga.

Lulip Muorahisčohkka

Contemplating the way across the Šielmmánjira River

TJÄKTJA STF FJÄLLSTUGA (1015M)

Built in 1984 to reduce the distance between Alesjaure and Sälka, Tjäktja is the highest *fjällstuga* on the Kungsleden; it is also one of the smallest. The *fjällstuga* is set at the foot of Lulip Muorahisčohkka's dark cliffs and consequently the site has a very Alpine feel to it. Tjäktja also offers good opportunities for observing wildlife – wolverine, arctic fox and reindeer are frequent visitors, especially at dawn and dusk. The chances of sightings are undoubtedly bolstered by the presence nearby of a natural feeding station used by arctic fox.

Facilities are limited to a single communal cabin with beds for 20 and a *tältservicestuga* for campers. There is no *bastu* or shop on site although the *stugvärdar* can provide weather forecasts. Numerous good camp spots are found 100m north of the buildings. Bank cards can be used at Tjäktja. Views to the north from Tjäktja are extensive.

STAGE 4
Tjäktja to Sälka

Start	Tjäktja STF Fjällstuga 1015m
Finish	Sälka STF Fjällstuga 815m
Distance	12.5km
Ascent	115m
Descent	315m
Grade	Moderate
Time	4hr 30min
Terrain	High mountain pass followed by a short steep descent into a long u-shaped glacial valley
Shelter	Emergency shelter at Tjäktja Pass
Camping	Wild – some opportunities for wild camping once the descent from the Tjäktja Pass is complete. Also pitches around Sälka for those wishing to camp away from the *fjällstuga*. Paid – Sälka STF Fjällstuga
Resupply	Shop at Sälka STF Fjällstuga

At 1150m, the Tjäktja Pass is the highest point on the Kungsleden and it is rarely snow free, even in midsummer. When the weather is favourable many walkers elect to bypass Tjäktja STF Fjällstuga entirely and keep going over the pass and on to Sälka, a total of 25.6km. The climb to the pass is comfortable except for a short final climb to a well-positioned shelter. Once over the pass, breathtaking views southward are to be had of the Tjäktjavagge, the long glacial valley that will be followed all the way to Kaitumjaure 30km to the south. A short steep descent delivers you onto the valley floor for the final, and in places rocky, 7km to Sälka.

Depart Tjäktja, retracing the trail back across the bridge to the west bank of the **Čeavččanjire River**. Follow the trail markings southwards as it cuts across small boulder fields in gentle ascent; the Tjäktja Pass (Tjäktjapasset) will be clearly visible as a shallow V in the lowest point of the skyline ahead. Snow patches are common so keep following the (protruding) painted marker stones and the

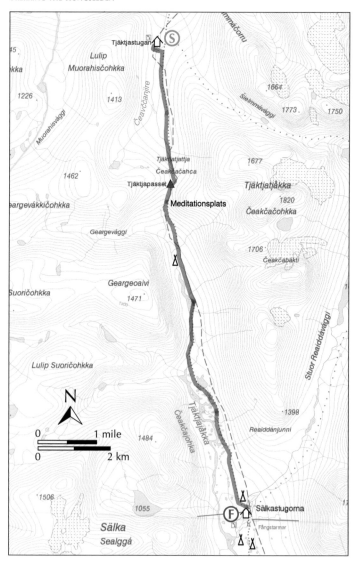

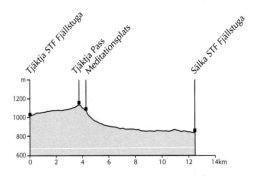

footprints of others; off to the left the line of winter trail markers makes a more direct line to the pass. Beware of straying too far right and encountering weak snow bridges over the upper reaches of the Čeavččanjire. Soon the shelter and final short steepening to the pass will be visible. Merge with the winter trail for this final climb.

Tjäktja Pass (1150m) – the emergency shelter at the Tjäktja Pass is the first of many such shelters encountered on the Kungsleden, all being provided by the local council which, in this instance is Norrbotten County. Thoughtfully located, such shelters provide a timely chance to rest and eat during the day's walk. At Tjäktja the shelter consists of three buildings that are all lashed down against strong winds. The shelter itself is wooden with a metal roof. Inside it is clean and equipped with an entrance hall leading into the communal area where there is a wood burner, table, benches and a shelf. Tools are provided such as snow shovel, wood axe, saw and floor brush. A very short way from the main building are a wood shed and a latrine. The walk up from Tjäktjastugan takes 90min so the shelter is a welcome opportunity to rest, escape the weather and chat to other walkers before the descent into Tjäktjavagge. One can only imagine what wind speeds and forces these exposed buildings have to endure during mountain storms!

Resume the trail and descend directly from the pass. ◀ The descent is steep in places and great care is required on one obvious 50m section, poles may be a great help, especially for probing any accumulations of snow. Keep an eye open for a **meditationsplats** just east of the trail during the descent. Follow the path along the valley floor. Here it is rocky and apart from where board-walks have been laid, progress will be slowed. Good

Spectacularly long views down into the u-shaped Tjäktjavagge Valley will be immediately apparent, the valley floor being hemmed in by steep sides, carved and truncated by long-gone glaciers.

Heading towards the Tjäktja Pass

camp spots are to be had where the trail draws level with the subsidiary Geargevággi Valley.

Continue south for 2km until the trail becomes less rocky and easier, meadow beginning to predominate over rock and stone. The trail parallels the **Tjäktjajåkka River** and camp spots are to be had in many places between the path and the river.

The Tjäktjavagge seen from the Tjäktja Pass

> The opposing sides of the **Tjäktjavagge Valley** have markedly different characteristics. The west side consists primarily of steep black cliffs and sweeping green talus (a scree that has been recolonised by vegetation). On the east side the slopes are far less steep and not having dark cliffs, seem far less ominous in character. This dissimilarity is primarily a product of the underlying geology. The west walls consist of hard resistant quartzite and limestone horizons which have contributed to the formation of rich meadows down below on the valley floor. By contrast, the east side, lacking in rich carbonates, is far sparser in terms of vegetation; the easier

83

angled slopes being a direct function of the dip (or slope) of the underlying bedding planes.

Although the *fjällstuga* at Sälka (**Sälkastugorna**) sits on a small rise, it remains hidden from sight by an intervening ridge until late in the day; this can make the last few kilometres seem drawn out. Don't let this detract from the grand settings. The odd glance backwards will reward you with views of the spectacular scenery that has been traversed during the preceding hours during the final approach to the fjällstuga.

SÄLKA STF FJÄLLSTUGA (815M)

The elevated collection of buildings at Sälka occupy a picturesque location on the meadows of the valley floor. The first building on the site was a small Sámi *kåta* built in 1909. It remains to this day, unmistakable by virtue of its pyramidal design; this shape has also earned them the name *prisma*. In all there are beds for 53 across three cabins. There is a dedicated area for dog owners, and those camping on site have a dedicated *tältservicestuga*. There are plentiful good camp spots close to both the buildings and the nearby stream; the pitches are on grass and are flat, level and dry. Sälka boasts a *bastu* and a well-stocked shop which accepts cards as well as cash. Weather forecasts are available. Fresh eggs are sometimes sold by the shop if there has been a helicopter service in recently.

STAGE 5
Sälka to Singi

Start	Sälka STF Fjällstuga 815m
Finish	Singi STF Fjällstuga 720m
Distance	11.6km
Ascent	70m
Descent	165m
Grade	Easy
Time	4hr 20min
Terrain	Gently undulating descent along glacial valley floor
Shelter	Emergency shelter at Kuoperjåkka
Camping	Wild – save for spots south of and close to Sälka, poor initially as the trail climbs away from the river. Opportunities for camping improve in the second half of the stage. Paid – Singi STF Fjällstuga
Resupply	Nil

A second day spent in the spectacular Tjäktjavagge Valley. This relatively short stage has no major climbs, is not particularly rocky and as such, makes for an easy day on the trail. The valley gradually opens up to the south providing spectacular scenery in every direction. Many pass straight through or bypass Singi making for Kebnekaise to the east (see Additional itinerary 1), or continue southwards to Kaitumjaure, the next STF *fjällstuga* on the Kungsleden.

Pick up the trail southwards from Sälka passing many good camp spots over the next 2km. The path remains level and slowly closes with the Tjäktjajåkka. Following 3km of walking, cross two metal suspension bridges in short succession that span the braided outflow of the Gaskkasjohka River. Continue, climbing gently and pass through a **reindeer fence**. ▸ Ascend a little higher to reach a **meditationsplats** from where there are good views across the Tjäktjavagge and up into the Čuhčavággi Valley. Follow the gently descending path to another metal suspension bridge that spans a ravine cut by the

This fence marks the boundary between the Leavas and Norrkaitum Sámi lands.

85

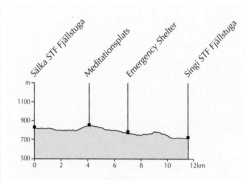

The view up the Guobirvággi to the northeast will reveal the jagged ridge of the Drakryggen (dragon's back).

Guobirjohka River. ◄ Cross the bridge and continue southwards, still descending, towards an emergency shelter that can be clearly seen a short distance ahead at **Kuoperjåkka** (760m). The shelter is of the same design and layout as the previous shelter at the Tjäktja Pass although not tethered. The location commands fantastic views in all directions and is a wonderful place to rest and spend some time observing the reindeer and waterfowl that are

Shelter at Kuoperjåkka

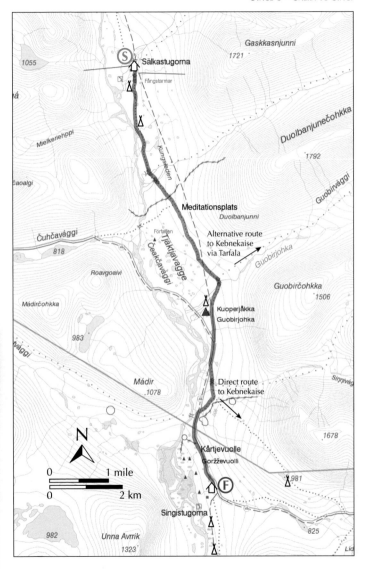

common in the area. Many good camp spots are to be found just off the trail between the bridge and shelter.

Alternative route to Kebnekaise
(Abisko-Nikkaluokta circuit)

Just prior to the bridge that spans the Guobirjohka, a path departs the Kungsleden and heads off in a northeast direction up into the Guobirvággi Valley. This path will eventually lead, after a spectacular and remote 14km, to the Tarfala STF Fjällstuga. From Tarfala it is a few hours walk to Kebnekaise fjällstation. The Tarfala route offers a more mountainous and remote alternative than going via Singi for those undertaking the Abisko-Nikkaluokta circuit.

Here the river is broad and slow-flowing with islets and gravel banks.

Continue southwards in gentle descent, closing in once again with the Tjäktjajåkka. ◄ Across the valley the banded dark cliffs of Mádir (1078m) fall vertically to flat green meadows. Bear away from the river once again, cross another bridge and climb gently to a path junction with signposts. Those taking the Kungsleden should follow the signs for Singistugorna (3km) and Kaitumjaurestugorna (16km).

The direct route to Kebnekaise bypasses Singi STF Fjällstuga

Direct route to Kebnekaise (Abisko-Nikkaluokta circuit)
From the path junction it is possible to bypass Singi and make for Kebnekaise Fjällstation directly (14km) where you can connect with the main route of the Abisko-Nikkaluokta circuit (see Additional itinerary 1). Those bypassing Singi in favour of Kebnekaise should note there is a very good camp spot by the lake at 981m.

Descend a short distance from the path junction and pass close to a **reindeer fence**. ▶ Continue descending parallel with the fence, through some shoulder-high willow thickets and pass close to a ravine through which the Tjäktjajåkka narrows. Follow the trail onwards with grand views down onto flat meadows, the delta, and the Norrkaitum Sámi summer village, all of which are framed by the mighty and imposing bulks of Unna Avrrik (1323m) and Stuor Avrrik (1354m). Follow the somewhat stony trail for the final 2km to Singi STF Fjällstuga (**Singistugorna**). In contrast, there are smooth sections where the path encounters smooth glacially polished bedrock.

Take a glimpse back north at this point as this is the last opportunity for unimpeded views back up the mighty Tjäktjavagge.

SINGI STF FJÄLLSTUGA (720M)

Singi occupies a rocky and elevated position above the Tjäktjajåkka delta and is an important crossroads. From Singi one can continue southwards on the Kungsleden or head eastwards for Kebnekaise Fjällstation (14km) and Nikkaluokta (33km). Many walkers pass through Singi for various reasons; lack of a shop and *bastu*, the poor camping on site, 'Kebnekaise fixation' or the fact that Sälka and Kaitumjaure can be easily linked in a single day.

The first building at Singi was a *prisma* erected in 1929. Today it comprises another four buildings with beds for 49 which includes a separate room for those with dogs. The camping nearby (between the *fjällstuga* and the river) is poor due to the rocky nature of the ground. Those staying can pay by card as well as cash although there is no shop or *bastu* on site. *Stugvärdar* can provide local weather forecasts as well as forecasts for Kebnekaise summit. This is particularly useful for those heading east and planning an ascent of the mountain in the coming days. Those wishing to wild camp can find many good trailside spots south of Singi.

STAGE 6
Singi to Kaitumjaure

Start	Singi STF Fjällstuga 720m
Finish	Kaitumjaure STF Fjällstuga 620m
Distance	12.2km
Ascent	55m
Descent	155m
Grade	Easy
Time	4hr 30min
Terrain	Continued gradual descent along glacial valley floor, slightly steeper to finish through birch forest
Shelter	Nil
Camping	Wild – many small spots south of Singi. Some spots just prior to Kaitumjaure. Good spots 100m south of Kaitumjaure towards the lakeside. Paid – Kaitumjaure STF Fjällstuga
Resupply	Shop at Kaitumjaure STF Fjällstuga

This third and final day spent descending the Tjäktjavagge Valley is both short and comfortable. Many walkers will have chosen to turn off the Kungsleden at Singi and as a result the trail south of Singi will feel much less busy in terms of human traffic. Beyond Stuor-Jiertá the Tjäktjavagge enters its lower reaches and as it does so, it loses some of its dramatic impact. This is more than compensated for by the new and stunning vistas across Padje Kaitumjaure Lake which will be seen at the day's end. Many time-conscious walkers will complete this stage and the previous (Sälka to Singi) in a single 23.8km push. Kaitumjaure STF Fjällstuga enjoys one of the finest settings on the entire Kungsleden.

Head southwards from the *stugvärd*'s building and cross the nearby stream, continue southwards. The going is easy as it undulates and weaves through willow thicket, small moraines and trapped pools of water; many small camp spots exist along this stretch. Ahead, the twin bulks of **Stuor-Jiertá** (1543m) and **Stuor Avrrik** (1354m) stand

like sentinels and dominate the view; the two peaks force a narrowing in the Tjäktjavagge through which the trail and river converge.

Once beyond the confines of the 'stuors', keep following the trail southwards. The landscape is now softer and less stark than previously consisting of easier angled

View back north over the Tjäktjajåkka bridge

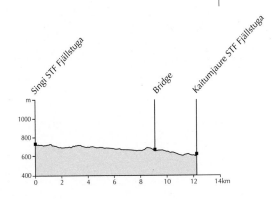

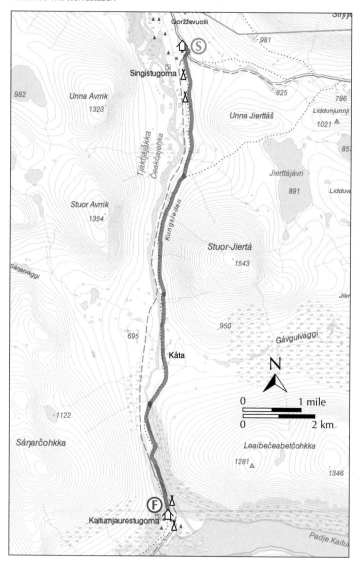

fellside in contrast to the rocks and cliffs of before. Cross an open flat area where the skeleton of an old *kåta* stands forlorn beside the trail. ▶ This flat area is where the Tjäktjavagge is met by the Gávgulvággi Valley coming in from the east; the vast spaciousness of the area far exceeds what one would expect from a modestly sized plain such as this.

The *kåta*'s covering is long gone and the structure now provides no shelter whatsoever.

South of the plain, ascend gently then more steeply, up and over a shoulder on the hillside. From the crest of the climb, look down on the Tjäktjajåkka narrowing and entering a deep gorge. Descend from the crest through sparse birch and take the bridge across to the west side of the gorge. Climb very briefly from the bridge then follow the trail as it traces the open hillside before descending into the birch treeline which is rich in grasses and star mosses.

Continue along the undulating trail taking time to enjoy the expanding views that open up ahead, a world away from the Tjäktjavagge and its steep black cliffs. The STF fjällstuga (**Kaitumjaurestugorna**) will hove into sight five minutes after the lake is first seen.

The descent to Kaitumjaure is dominated by **Padje Kaitumjaure Lake** which stretches off, seemingly without end, eastwards into the far distance. The entire lake is ringed by steep hillsides that plunge straight into the water. The highest of the surrounding peaks, Livamčohkka on the southern shore, towers to a height of 1481m. Down below the *fjällstuga* the lake forms a lush verdant delta where moose can sometimes be seen grazing in the marsh grasses.

KAITUMJAURE STF FJÄLLSTUGA (620M)

The original 1915 peat *kåta* can still be seen besides the *stugvärd*'s cabin at Kaitumjaure although it is no longer in use. The original intent for establishing a *fjällstuga* at Kaitumjaure was to make the trek between Kebnekaise and Sjöfallet a reality. At that time a boat was also provided for crossing the Padje Kaitumjaure.

Sunshine and snow at Kaitumjaure STF Fjällstuga

Today the *fjällstuga* consists of two main buildings with beds for 30. Small comfortable camp spots are dotted around the site and campers share the facilities with others. Those staying off site can also find good pitches down on the open ground besides the delta. There are two *bastu* on site although the older one, despite being serviceable, is no longer used. The shop is well-stocked and cards can be used as well as cash. *Stugvärdar* will provide weather forecasts and there is also information posted concerning the motorised crossings in both directions; Alisjávri to the north (Stage 2) and at Teusajaure to the south (Stage 8).The buildings at Kaitumjaure are ideally positioned for catching the morning sun and have outside decking, benches and chairs for this purpose. What better than to eat your breakfast in the warm sun while you soak up the incredible surroundings and views, maybe spotting individual moose grazing down on the delta.

The older of the two *bastur* is cleverly built astride a small stream. A hatch in the floor allows users to access fresh water for heating and washing without having to pre-stock nor fetch mid-sauna. The sauna was last used by the *stugvärdar* and to this day it is still in excellent condition despite being no longer in use.

STAGE 7
Kaitumjaure to Teusajaure

Start	Kaitumjaure STF Fjällstuga 620m
Finish	Teusajaure STF Fjällstuga 500m
Distance	8.6km
Ascent	200m
Descent	320m
Grade	Easy
Time	3hr 30min
Terrain	Spacious open fell then finishing in a picturesque lakeside setting
Shelter	Nil
Camping	Wild – camping is possible virtually anywhere above the treeline although, season depending, water isn't always to hand, so choose carefully. Paid – Teusajaure STF Fjällstuga
Resupply	Shop at Teusajaure STF Fjällstuga

This is one of the shortest days on the Kungsleden and makes for an easy and enjoyable walk through part of the 2850km² Sjaunja Nature Reserve, one of two such nature reserves within the Laponian UNESCO World Heritage Area. Sleeping in and starting later than normal might be a good way to begin this day. The landscape is now softer and more open, a complete contrast to that of the past few days. The day finishes with a short, steep descent to Teusajaure whose lakeside location and scenery put even Kaitumjaure to shame.

Follow the signposted path downhill from the *fjällstuga* through birch forest. ▶ **Stone markers replace the red paint** on this stage and the path is easily followed. Continue for 30min to arrive at the roaring **Kaitumjåkka River** which flows fast and broiling through a shallow ravine, cross the metal suspension bridge to the south bank and continue parallel and close to the frothing waters. Small camp spots can be found hereabouts by the river's edge.

En route keep an eye open for moose grazing on the delta or even closer as at times the trail passes close to the fertile marshes.

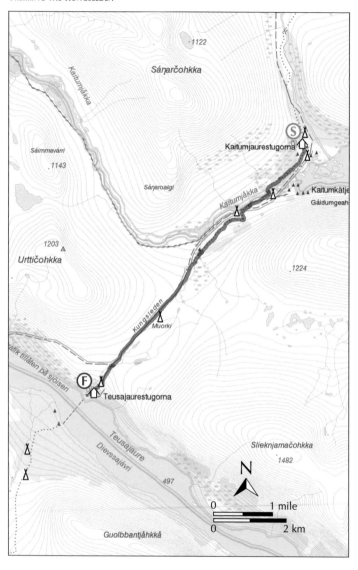

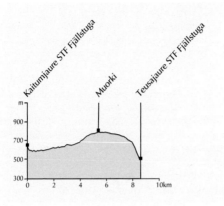

Follow the rocky trail whose markers consist of small cairns and upright slabs. Some 500m beyond the bridge a **reindeer fence** and gate are reached. Pass through the gate and continue on, skirting a small lake where nearby, on elevated ground, small camp spots can be found. Follow the trail which steepens briefly and brings you to an area where pools have formed in the hollows between glacial mounds; beyond these the trail and river part company, the river bearing away from the trail in a long bend to the northwest.

Keep following the trail southwestwards as it begins its long easy ascent across the vast open fellside towards the Muorki plateau/saddle. The path cuts through dwarf birch and willow on the way up, sometimes over board-walks, but never with difficulty. Markers are still few and far between, the paint being faint, but fortunately the trail is easily followed. ▶ Mount a final short steepening to reach **Muorki**. The saddle is broad and open and its fine views make for a great lunch stop in fine weather. The flat saddle has good camp spots although water is limited to a small lake.

The **view** southwards has yet to reveal the Teusa Valley in all its glory although it does offer a

Note how Slieknjamačohkka (1482m) to the southeast appears in profile like a breaking wave.

glimpse of the next day's terrain – another high fell plateau. Further south again and if the weather permits, snowy mountain tops will be seen. This will be your first glimpse of Sarek's majestic and famous mountains.

The next stage begins with a mandatory boat crossing: the motorised service operates at 0700 and 1600, with an additional 1800 service in mid-summer, or you can use the STF rowing boats.

Cross the saddle southwestwards for 1km before beginning the descent towards the Teusa Valley. The slope is gently convex and steepens as progress is made. Cross a small metal bridge, **being careful not to follow the winter markers westwards**. Five minutes later, where the trail steepens, an unnamed river crashes and tumbles over an edge; follow the rocky trail into the birch forest. **Teusajaure Lake** will now be clearly visible through gaps in the trees and hopefully, if the sun is shining, glittering beneath a deep blue sky. A good small camp spot is passed in the trees for those not wishing to stay at the STF *fjällstuga* (**Teusajaurestugorna**) otherwise, continue descending through the birch to the lake's edge where the fjällstuga is perfectly situated. ◄

The Muorki plateau/saddle, Slieknjamačohkka's wave-like profile is just visible

The view southeastwards along Teusajaure

TEUSAJAURE STF FJÄLLSTUGA (500M)

The first building was established by the STF at Teusajaure in 1909 but as early as 1918, was already in need of major repairs. Upgrades have been a continuous process ever since with the latest addition being a *bastu* in 2004. The *fjällstuga*'s lakeside setting is one of the very finest on the Kungsleden – when viewed from here, the Teusa Valley is simply breathtaking. The opportunity to soak in this amazing landscape should not to be passed up by rushing through. The *fjällstuga* has a well-stocked shop and a dedicated room and kitchen for those with dogs. Campers share facilities with everyone else and there is bed space for up to 30. Although the shop does accept cards, it does not, in contrast to many other *fjällstugor*, accept Euros or Norwegian Krone. Small camp spots are scattered around the buildings and on the edge of the trees by the lake shore.

STAGE 8
Teusajaure to Saltoluokta via Vakkotavare

Start	Teusajaure STF Fjällstuga 500m
Finish	Vakkotavare STF Fjällstuga 470m
Distance	13.7km walking (plus 1km boat crossing)
Ascent	480m
Descent	510m
Grade	Moderate
Time	4hr 50min (walking)
Terrain	Lake crossing, open fell and birch forest
Shelter	Dievssajávri rest cabin on south shore of Teusajaure
Camping	Wild – many opportunities for wild camping above the treeline. Paid – Vakkotavare STF Fjällstuga and Saltoluokta Fjällstation
Resupply	Shop at Vakkotavare STF Fjällstuga. Comprehensive shop and facilities at Saltoluokta if travelling that far

This, the final stage of the Kungsleden's northern section is very similar in character to the previous day although longer. As Teusajaure is crossed at the day's start, Sjaunja Nature Reserve is left behind and the Stora Sjöfallets National Park entered. Following a steep climb on to the plateau the walker will be rewarded with magnificent views of the Sarek peaks which now appear in all their snow-capped glory. A steep and rocky final descent to the *fjällstuga* at Vakkotavare completes the walking. Most will travel onwards by bus and ferry to Saltoluokta if continuing southwards, or to Gällivare if departing the Kungsleden. If travelling onward from Vakkotavare be sure to arrive in time for the last bus of the day.

At Teusajaure you come to the first mandatory boat crossing on the Kungsleden. These crossings undoubtedly add colour and adventure to the overall experience but also require planning ahead if you have a schedule to keep. At Teusajaure the crossing can be made either by using the rowing boats provided by the STF (20min at best, 60min if you have to cross three times in order to return a boat)

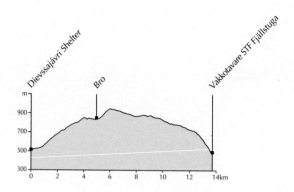

or the *in situ* STF motorised service (which takes a mere two minutes) operated by the *stugvärd* of the *fjällstuga*. Weather permitting, the lake can be rowed across at any time and many will make this journey at the day's end, camping on the south shore so as to make a prompt start the next day.

Motorised crossings are at 0700, 1600 and 1800 daily. Although the boat can only carry four passengers, it will keep ferrying until everyone waiting is across. Those on the opposite south shore should raise the barrel on the pole provided to indicate they are waiting for the service. Costs are SEK100 each way for STF members, SEK150 for non-members. Members under 16 travel free, non-members for SEK50. From the first Monday in September until the season's end, scheduled crossings are reduced to the 0700 and 1600 service only.

Pick up the trail into the birch forest then climb for a few minutes to a sign for the Dievssajávri *raststuga* or rest cabin located 75m left of the path. This small wooden cabin is simply equipped with benches, table and a wood burner. A double latrine stands close by. The surrounding ground is rocky and unsuitable for camping. Continue on a steady ascent with short steep sections in places. There are only a few faint trail markers painted on the trees,

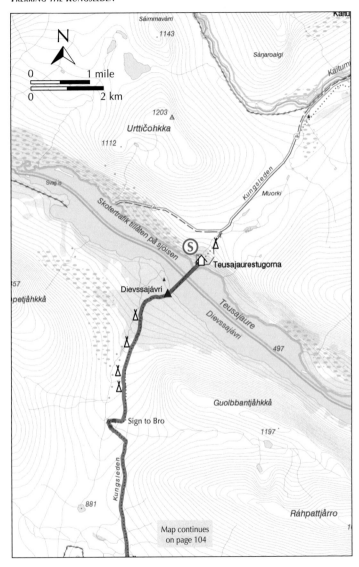

Map continues
on page 104

STORA SJÖFALLETS NATIONAL PARK

On Teusajaure's south shore, the Stora Sjöfallets National Park is announced by a noticeboard. With an area of 1278 km², Stora Sjöfallet is the third-largest national park in Sweden. The main reason for the park's foundation in 1909 was the magnificent Stour Muorkkegårttje waterfall. Soon after the area was given its protected status however, the Swedish government permitted hydroelectric development which deprived the falls of most of their water flow and affected the shorelines of nearby Akkajaure. Later developments included power lines, roads, and gravel banks. In the 1960s the status as national park was called into question due to these severe changes and today the area of the falls is sadly no longer part of the national park.

however the path is obvious and easily followed. After 30min ascent a good camp spot is passed in the trees with space for four tents, water can be sourced from the nearby Gáppejåhkå River. ▸ Continue climbing moderately steeply until you exit the treeline some 45min from the lakeshore. Now out on the open fell, markers become more frequent. Continue climbing southwards on a good trail that parallels the Gáppejåhkå, passing many pleasant camp spots on the way.

Plentiful bilberry can be seen during the ascent from the lake.

The climb eases on a rocky section of trail just below a brow. From here, follow the small 'Bro' (bridge) **sign** right and downhill to the river crossing. The old trail, which is still obvious, used to continue straight ahead where the sign sits. **Do not be tempted to follow the old trail** as it leads to a waded crossing of the same river that the new bridge now makes easier. The rerouting does involve additional descent and re-ascent but it is worth the small effort. Once across the bridge, continue back uphill eastwards and before long, resume the southward heading once again. Still gently ascending, follow the path to a highpoint of 920m at the foot of the broad western ridge of **Ráhpattjårro** (1677m). ▸ Descend effortlessly across the open fell following the now numerous markers and boardwalks, good camp spots are to be found everywhere.

From here the Sarek peaks can be seen forming a jagged skyline in the distance.

Sarek's peaks can be seen once the open fell is reached.

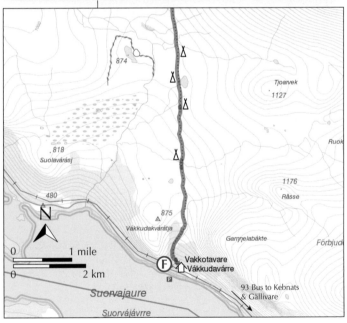

Continue southwards past a lake whereafter the trail begins to descend more purposefully to a small metal bridge. A pair of lonely reindeer herders' cabins will be seen on a rise off to the west as well as Suorvajaure Lake way down in the valley bottom.

Cross the bridge, gently ascending the trail to a meeting with a river and enter the birch forest for the final steep section. Carefully descend the trail as it weaves its way between **Vákkudakvárátja** (875m) and **Garŋŋelabákte**, twisting and turning through and over boulders in the forest. Finally, cross a wooden bridge and walk more easily the final few minutes to the STF fjällstuga at **Vakkotavare**.

VAKKOTAVARE STF FJÄLLSTUGA (470M)

The roadside *fjällstuga* at Vakkotavare commands excellent views out across the expansive Suorvajaure Lake, although the effect is slightly marred by the overhead power lines. The *fjällstuga* contains beds for 18 and camp spots are located across the road and down by the lake. The *fjällstuga* has no *bastu* although there is a shop that accepts cards as well as Euro and Norwegian Krone. There is a payphone on site, which is just as well as the Telia network is the only mobile signal available. Campers share the facilities of the rearmost

Descending towards Vakkotavare

cabin, while dog owners have a dedicated room for themselves. Out front, overlooking the lake and the road is a raised area of wooden decking with benches and tables, a perfect place to sit and chat with other walkers as you wait for the bus. The Number 93 bus stop is located on the road immediately in front of the *fjällstuga*. Most walkers plan to arrive at Vakkotavare in time to catch the bus, with very few planning a stay overnight at the STF *fjällstuga*.

ONWARD TRAVEL

The break in the Kungsleden at Vakkotavare is filled by means of 27km of road and an STF ferry across Langas Lake to Saltoluokta (3.5km). Although it is possible to walk along the road to Kebnats and catch the ferry, very few choose to do so. The number 93 bus operates between Gällivare in the east (3hr 30min) and Ritsem STF Fjällstuga in the west (50min). Between mid-June and the end of August the 93 departs Vakkotavare eastwards at 1450 with an additional departure at 1105 operating throughout July, August and September. Up-to-date timetables can be found at www.ltnbd.se/en/timetables.

If you're departing the Kungsleden at Vakkotavare, take the 93 bus all the way to Gällivare from where onward travel by air, train, road and bus is easily facilitated. If you're continuing on the Kungsleden you should also catch the 93 bus towards Gällivare and alight at Kebnats (1hr) where the waiting STF ferry will take you across to Saltoluokta STF Fjällstation (10min).

The bus only accepts cards as payment for the SEK78 one-way journey to Kebnats. The ferry cost to Saltoluokta is SEK140 for STF members and SEK200 for non-members; SEK120 and SEK180 respectively for under-26s. Ferry schedules are synchronised with the 93 bus arrival at Kebnats and deliver you directly across Langas Lake to the *fjällstation* at Saltoluokta.

En route to Kebnats the 93 bus makes a 30min stop at Stora Sjöfallet Mountain Centre where soft drinks, ice cream and a very limited selection of stores are available; the total travel time to Kebnats including this stop is 1hr.

ADDITIONAL ITINERARIES

ADDITIONAL ITINERARY 1
Singi to Nikkaluokta (alternative finish to Section 1)

Start	Singi STF Fjällstuga 720m
Finish	Nikkaluokta 480m
Distance	32km
Ascent	330m
Descent	570m
Grade	Moderate
Time	2 days
Accommodation	Camping or STF *fjällstation*

Combined with Stages 1–5, this itinerary completes the justifiably popular Abisko to Nikkaluokta circuit, a 103km loop that represents an uncomplicated week's walking through some of the Kungsleden's very best scenery. With Kiruna as the point of access, transport links in and out are straightforward and numerous. STF services are good and offer security to those who are venturing out maybe for the first time. For those seeking a measure of solitude, meanwhile, quiet spots are easily found for wild camping in the evenings when the trail gets quiet.

DAY 1
Singi to Kebnekaise

Start	Singi STF Fjällstuga 720m
Finish	Kebnekaise STF Fjällstation 660m
Distance	14.1km
Ascent	200m
Descent	260m
Grade	Moderate
Time	5hr
Terrain	Open fell and deep mountain valley
Shelter	Nil
Camping	Wild – many opportunities on the open fell. Free – Kebnekaise STF Fjällstation
Resupply	Shop at Kebnekaise STF Fjällstation

This, the first of two days linking Singi with Nikkaluokta, takes in some extremely imposing and beautiful mountain scenery. Kebnekaise itself remains largely hidden, although this does not detract from the overall experience. On departing the Kungsleden at Singi the red paint markers cease, although the path remains well defined and easy to follow in the main. Kebnekaise STF Fjällstation, a very busy destination in season, will not be to everyone's taste or liking.

From the outset the chiselled form of Liddubákti (1759m) will dominate the view ahead.

Hanging streams tumble from the heights above the trail.

Following Kebnekaise signs, depart Singi gently ascending along a path heading eastwards, do not cross the stream in pursuit of the winter markers. ◀ Continue for 40min until you reach a long thin lake where there are good camp spots. Still ascending, pass around the north shore of the lake and continue for another 30min to a highpoint on a shoulder with good camp spots, again besides a nearby lake. Liddubákti, now much closer, appears massive and immovable, guarding the entrance to the Láddjurvaggi valley that lies ahead. ◀

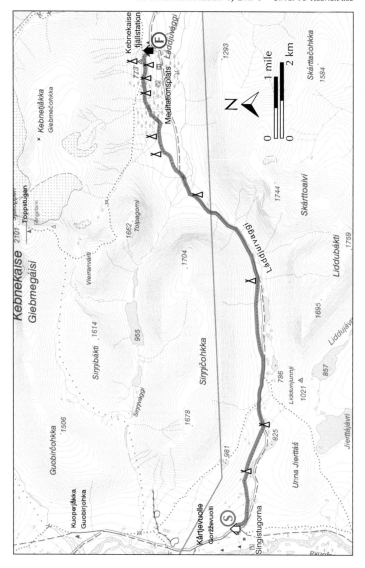

Liddubákti seen en route from Singi

Continue over slightly rockier terrain (with winter markers for company) and follow the trail as it begins its descent towards the valley floor. The odd snow patch may be encountered on the path even in midsummer, although these should cause no problem. Continue through the **Láddjurvaggi**, passing a series of small lakes where there is much camping potential; the winter trail passes very close to these lakes, while the summer path remains on a slightly elevated and parallel course. Continue past a longer lake and near its outflow converge once again with the winter markers.

This is where the valley is at its most striking with precipitous walls and red scree fans rising to more than 1500m. Many classic **glacial features** will be on this section of the path such as glacially striated rock, erratic boulders, hanging streams and truncated cirques high up above the cliffs.

Continue along the now very flat valley bottom, making sure to keep left so as to pass close by a pile of extremely large cubic rocks; this will ensure you stay out of the very marshy ground close to the river. The towering masses of **Siŋŋičohkka** (1704m) and **Tolpagorni** (1662m) dominate along this stretch of path and good camp spots are to be had on the flat valley at their base. Cross a bridge made of logs and enter an area of willow thicket where the path weaves around, but ultimately keeps to a northeastwards course; planks will assist with the identification of the correct way to go. Cross a second log bridge marking the thicket's end; here the winter markers will be 200m to your right. Ahead lies a low-profiled rock mound, head straight towards this and cross it at its left-hand extreme, noting the very clear and distinct glacial striations scoured into the rock.

This large rock feature is a very good example of a **rôche moutonnée** (or sheepback). These are created by the passage of a glacier resulting in asymmetric erosion. The steep upstream face is referred to as the 'stoss' and the shallower downstream side as the 'lee'.

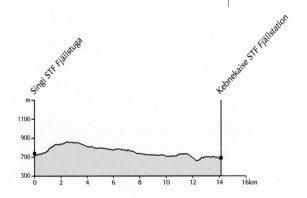

Five minutes beyond the rôche, crest a rocky top from where there are much expanded views eastwards that includes sight of the mast at the *fjällstation*. Also, take a moment to look northwestwards up into the Kittelbäcken where Sydtoppen (2098m), Kebnekaise's summit is located. Many camp on the flat meadows adjacent to the mouth of the Kittelbäcken. From the crest, descend to and cross a metal suspension bridge passing the sixth **meditationsplats** of the Dag Hammarskjöld Way en route. Once across the metal bridge, climb steeply to cross a wooden bridge whereafter the going eases. Follow the rocky path as it contours along the hillside passing many (probably occupied) camp spots. A thicket of tall birch and a vertical rock face announce that Kebnekaise Fjällstation is but 5min walk away.

Wild campers at the mouth of the Kittelbäcken: Kebnekaise summit is at the far right partially obscured by cloud

KEBNEKAISE STF FJÄLLSTATION (660M)

Kebnekaise STF Fjällstation viewed from the east

This *fjällstation* is used by the experienced and inexperienced alike as their base for ascending Kebnekaise. Being only a day's walk from Nikkaluokta it gets very busy in season, especially at weekends. Many who can afford to fly in and out on helicopters, and at times the buzz from them is almost constant. Little surprise then that the facilities are comprehensive and impersonal. Many room types are available and although there are 190 beds, booking is advised in season, essential at weekends.

Camping is free at the *fjällstation*, although tents must be pitched 300m or more away from the buildings. Good spots abound, although they are soon filled; a good flat and quiet spot can be found 150m north of the 773m spot height and is accessed by a short steep climb from the main building – a sufficient deterrent, it seems, for most campers! A service fee of SEK315 (SEK215 for STF members) is charged for 24-hour use of the facilities in the *servishus* which contains showers, *bastu*, large kitchen and dining room, drying room, weather forecasts and a guiding services desk. There is free Wi-Fi on site, although phone signal is also good. Reception is located in the main building and is open 0600–2200. Guiding for Kebnekaise summit is available via the desk in the *servishus* for around SEK1500 per person. The shop in the main building is more limited than that at Abisko, although it has some fuel, dehydrated trekking food as well as more bulky food items. The *fjällstation* serves an excellent all-you-can-eat breakfast from 0600 onwards.

113

DAY 2
Kebnekaise to Nikkaluokta

Start	Kebnekaise STF Fjällstation 660m
Finish	Nikkaluokta 480m
Distance	17.9km
Ascent	130m
Descent	310m
Grade	Moderate
Time	6hr
Terrain	Airy birch forest
Shelter	Simple wooden hut at Láddjujávri boat jetty
Camping	Wild – periodic opportunities as far as Láddjujávri village
Resupply	Enoks café at Láddjujávri village

An enjoyable stage in the Láddjuvággi to complete the Abisko to Nikkaluokta circuit. Much of the time will be spent in the airy birch forest, which does restrict the views ahead somewhat. The trail, which is rocky to begin, widens and becomes easier going as it approaches Nikkaluokta. For those that wish, a boat service across Láddjujávri will shave 7km of walking off the distance.

From the fjällstation follow signs for Nikkaluokta that take boardwalks past the **helipad** and into the spacious birch forest. At **Tarfalajokk** the Darfáljohka roars through a gorge. Cross the metal suspension bridge and continue gently descending passing a sign indicating that it is 7km to the Láddjujávri boat jetty; every kilometre hereafter is similarly signposted. Tarfalajokk has a basic campsite with simple bench seating and a latrine.

The limited views ahead are of rounded soft hilltops and a verdant valley floor, a sure sign that the mountains are now behind you.

◀ Continue as the trail contours the hillside elevated above the valley bottom passing the occasional camp spot along the way. The first sight of Láddjujávri will be caught just before passing beneath the undercut cliffs of **Darfáloalgi**. Pass a small lake and the final *meditationsplats* in short succession as you walk parallel with a powerline

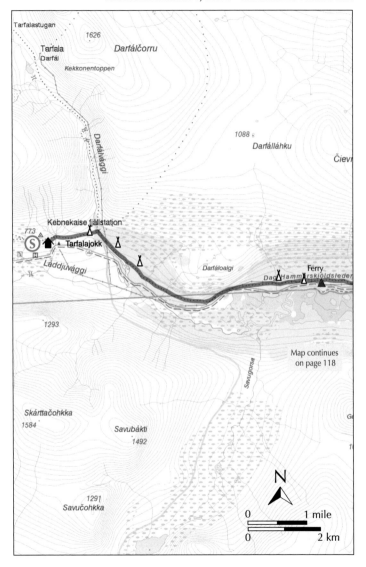

through a very scruffy section of the trail that includes a large level boulder field. You will now be entering prime moose country, open birch forest replete with lush marsh grasses besides the water's edge. Moose are prevalent in the area so it is worth keeping watch as you pass along.

Continue easily to the 1km sign for the ferry where excellent camp spots can be found on the left among the birch, where a stream flows nearby. Pass wetlands on the right to arrive at a sign announcing the ferry, which is a 100m detour from the trail and equipped with a simple wooded shelter, rubbish bin and a latrine.

The Láddjujávri ferry operates between here and Ladtjoluspekåtan some 7km to the east, offering an alternative route to the village. Prices are SEK350 for adults, SEK175 for under-16s and SEK100 for dogs. Five services run daily in each direction between 0915 and 1845 (tel 073 0317027/070 535 5666 or info@enoks.se).

Continue on the now noticeably less rocky trail as it parallels the delta and then **Láddjujávri** itself. Very easily now, cross open areas that afford views of the lake and also the cliffs and talus of **Gármasbákti** to the left, arriving soon after at **Ladtjoluspekåtan**.

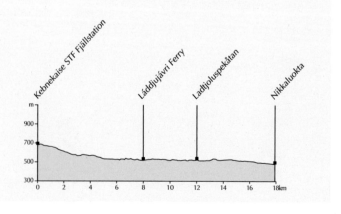

The view backwards across the Láddjuvággi wetlands

LADTJOLUSPEKÅTAN

Ladtjoluspekåtan is the eastern terminus of the ferry service and also home to the excellent Enoks café (1000 to 1800) (www.enoks.se/en) which serves snacks, dried reindeer meat and light meals as well as hot and cold drinks; chalet accommodation is also available on site. The modern wooden building is eye-catching and is very striking on the approach to the village. The café is named in honour of Enok Sarri whose parents were among the first settlers at Nikkaluokta in 1911. Enok's father, Nils Olsson Sarri, was the first director of Kebnekaise Fjällstation where he also served as a mountain guide. Enok Sarri followed in his father's footsteps and also became the SMHI's (Sveriges Meteorologiska och Hydrologiska Institut) weather observer in Nikkaluokta between 1950 and 1975. He augmented his official weather forecasting with traditional methods such as reading fish and reindeer ages.

Enok Sarri became a Swedish national celebrity in 1977 when he predicted that the king's firstborn would be a prince, promising to crawl from Nikkaluokta to Kiruna if his prediction was wrong. When the Princess Victoria was born, reporters discovered that the promise was easily delivered as Kiruna's border was just a few metres from Sarri's cabin in Nikkaluokta.

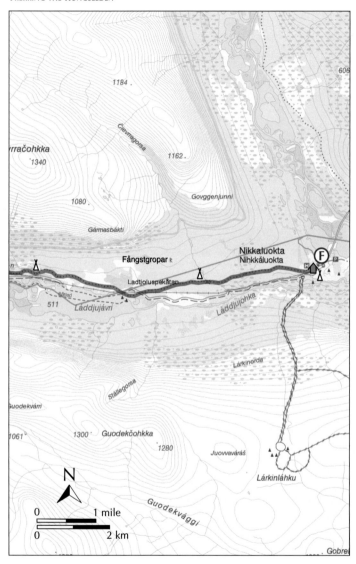

From Ladtjoluspekåtan, follow the wide and smooth trail onward through the birch passing a sign for the Fångstgropar which is a short diversion to the left.

The Fångstgropar are a system of disused **trapping pits** which the Sámi formerly used to hunt reindeer before herding became their prevalent way of life. Rows of pits were dug in soft sandy ground 3–4m in diameter and 2.5m deep. The pits were often camouflaged and the reindeer then driven towards them, once caught, the steep sides ensured that none could escape.

Continue and cross a bridge whereafter the trail is gravelled for over a kilometre before alternating back to smooth soil for the final short walk into **Nikkaluokta** where a pole arch awaits to mark the trail's end.

Trail's End at Nikkaluokta

ADDITIONAL ITINERARY 2
Kebnekaise summit

Start/finish	Kebnekaise STF Fjällstation 660m
Distance	17.4km
Ascent/descent	1720m
Grade	Challenging
Time	10hr (6hr ascent plus 4hr descent)
Terrain	Non-technical mountainous terrain
Maps	Calazo 1:15,000 Hög Alpin Karta Kebnekaise
Shelter	1983 Toppstugan 1854m (N7535029 E647352), 1962 Toppstugan 1873m (N7535061 E647519) (off main trail), 2017 Toppstugan 2040m (N7535751 E647463)
Marking	Very well marked with red paint throughout
Equipment	Weather forecast, map and compass, warm clothing, hat and gloves, windproof layer, food and drink, walking boots, sun protection, whistle, head torch, small emergency bivvy bag, spare high energy food
Water	Last reliable water at the Giebmejohka River although it is advisable to treat it before drinking
Notes	Mountain guide staff from the *fjällstation* patrol the route high on the mountain during peak periods in the summer. Although not essential, you may find walking poles of great benefit, especially during descent over rocky ground. The ascent is of a similar nature to that of Ben Nevis in the UK.

In favourable conditions an ascent of Kebnekaise (Sweden's highest peak at 2098m) makes for a rewarding and memorable experience. The Västra Leden (West Route) is non-technical and does not require specialist skills and equipment except for the very final section. However, one small turn in the weather can make a world of difference on any mountain, let alone one this high. Therefore, those attempting the summit should be certain that they are suitably informed, equipped and prepared. A defining characteristic of mountains is the rapid changeability of their weather; a good rule of thumb therefore is not to go beyond the point that you can easily reverse.

Timings are for a walker of average fitness with a small pack. The final summit consists of a short 75m climb on moderately inclined snow. This is easily negotiated without crampons and ice axe, although one slip could have disastrous consequences. Scaling this final section without such equipment is realistic only for those with experience of step-kicking in snow. If iced, crampons and ice axe are necessary for all. If you are determined to go to the summit, but are in any doubt, arrange to join a guided group from the *fjällstation*. The excellent and recommended Calazo Hög Alpin Karta Kebnekaise map is available to buy at the *fjällstation*.

Depart reception at the fjällstation and head westwards along the path that was used to come in on from Singi, this is also signposted for Kebnekaise summit. After 15min, follow an uphill branch that is signposted Västra Leden (West Route) and marked with red paint. Continue making an easy ascent across the fellside and cross two streams in short succession. Follow the trail into the **Kittelbäcken** gorge and climb the north bank steeply over rocky and loose ground for some time. Level out into a large rocky basin with views ahead to vertical rock faces and snow filled gullies, Kebnekaise is the right-hand solitary peak.

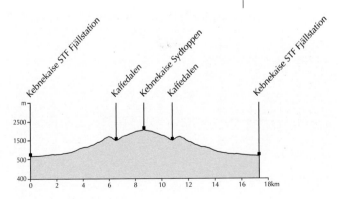

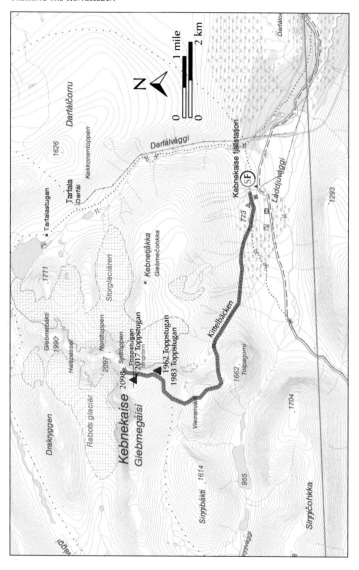

Cross the Giebmejohka River via a metal bridge and immediately begin climbing once again over large flagstones at the foot of a long slope. Smaller streams have to be negotiated just prior to the metal bridge – these can become full and require boots to be removed. The flagstones soon give way to rocky path and until late in the summer, a section of easy snowfield. As you near the top, **take care traversing a tricky section of piled blocks** before continuing to a brief respite on the rocky saddle between **Tolpagorni** (1662m) and **Vierranvárri** (1711m). ▸ Ascend steeply from the saddle up the rocky but well-bedded trail which attacks Vierranvárri's southern flank. After 30min, the angle relents and the path zigzags to the summit where many small rock cairns have been built by previous walkers.

As of summer 2018, work was underway to flagstone this area of piled blocks, the work being undertaken by Nepalese and Norwegians.

The summit of **Vierranvárri** is a good opportunity to take a rest and enjoy the fantastic views. It also offers the chance to scan the remainder of the route to Kebnekaise's Sydtoppen (2098m) which is directly opposite to the north. In between lies a descent into the Kaffedalen (1526m) followed by a long final climb onto Kebnekaise.

The view backward from halfway up Vierranvárri's southern flank

Kebnekaise summit (these climbers have ascended by a more technical route than the Västra Leden)

Descend the steep rocky trail down into the Kaffedalen and almost immediately begin the very steep ascent out. Continue steeply on the rocky trail for an hour to where the angle eases a little. Traverse to the right for 10min before a renewed steepening leads to a large wooden cabin, the **1983 Toppstugan** (Top Hut) (1854m). This section, between the Kaffedalen and the 1983 Toppstugan, is the longest and most sustained climb of the entire day.

Toppstugans – the 1983 Toppstugan consists of a main cabin and a latrine. The cabin is in a poor state of repair although *in extremis* it would provide shelter. The installation of the new 2017 Toppstugan renders the cabin obsolete and there are plans to dismantle it completely. A second Toppstugan, built in 1962, is located about 200m northeast (and off the main trail) of the 1983 cabin. The 1962 building is smaller, although in much better condition and much cleaner. The path between both is marked by a line of poles (*fångstarm*) to prevent walkers

1983 Toppstugan

getting lost in poor visibility. The intention is for the 1962 cabin to remain in place.

2017 Toppstugan

Kebnekaise summit and 2017 Toppstugan

From the 1983 cabin continue ascending over rocky ground before reaching the snowline where the angle eases somewhat. Climb across the easy angled snow for 20min to reach the new **2017 Toppstugan** (2040m).

2017 Toppstugan – an elevated wooden structure of pentagonal cross-section, the cabin is not intended for overnight stays and consequently has no wood stove. The interior is very basic, consisting only of bench seating for 21 people.

The unmistakable **Sydtoppen** (2098m), shaped like a shark's fin, is now 15min easy walk away. Approach the summit direct and then ascend to the top with care via the easier angled right-hand (southern) side, keeping left as you go up. On a clear day the views are extraordinary and make the effort of the ascent wholly worthwhile. Descend via the same route, remembering that it includes a section of steep ascent back onto the cairn-littered summit of Vierranvárri.

SECTION 2 –
SALTOLUOKTA
TO KVIKKJOKK

Crossing the Lájtávrre (Stage 11)

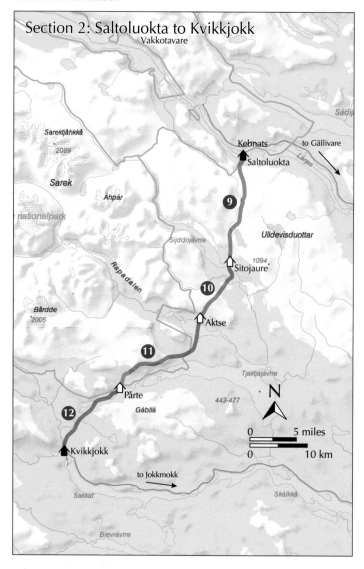

Section 2: Saltoluokta to Kvikkjokk

SECTION 2
Saltoluokta to Kvikkjokk

Start	Saltoluokta
Finish	Kvikkjokk
Distance	68.5km (walking distance 61.9km)
Ascent	1260m
Descent	1330m
Terrain	Fell and forest in near equal measure
High point	East flank of Njunjes 950m (Stage 10)
Boat crossings	Mandatory: Sitojaure and Lájtávrre (6.6km)

Now that the mountains are far behind, this second section consisting entirely of fell and forest will feel very different. The continuing provision of STF *fjällstugor* and excellent trail marking mean that it is popular with walkers, although not on the scale seen between Abisko and Vakkotavare. ▸

Though not as rugged and mountainous as the first section, the trail south of Saltoluokta is no less dramatic. No longer hemmed in by mountains, you will experience far greater and more expansive views when out on the open fell. Highlights include continuing views of the snowy Sarek Mountains, Skierffe's chiselled profile, the multi-hued Lájtávrre delta and the eerie Rittak Valley. For those wild camping there are opportunities to camp in some truly amazing locations on the open fell.

Transport in and out of Kvikkjokk can be challenging and requires careful prior planning.

Access
Gällivare, the hub for Saltoluokta, is serviced by both SJ trains and Nordica direct flights from Stockholm. From Gällivare, you can catch the 93 bus and alight at Kebnats for the STF ferry across to Saltoluokta and onto Section 2 of the Kungsleden. After Kebnats the 93 bus will continue on to Vakkotavare and allow access to Section 1 of the Kungsleden for those travelling northwards.

The STF ferry which links Kebnats and Saltoluokta is timetabled so as to meet **all** 93 bus services at Kebnats.

Full and up-to-date ferry information can be obtained from the *fjällstation* and can also be found online (www. swedishtouristassociation.com/learn/boats-in-the-mountains). Buses depart Kebnats for Vakkotavare at 1040 (mid-June to end of August) and 1500 (July, August and September). For Gällivare, buses depart at 1615 (mid-June to end of August) and 1230 (July, August and September).

Kvikkjokk sits at a remote roadhead linked by the 47 bus to Jokkmokk. From Jokkmokk a 44 bus will take you to Gällivare or alternatively, a 43 bus will take you to Murjek from where the SJ train network can be accessed.

Maps
- 1:75,000 Outdoorkartan Blad 3 (Saltoluokta-Padjelanta-Kvikkjokk) OR
- 1:100,000 Fjällkartan BD10 (Sarek Nationalpark) OR
- 1:100,000 Calazo Fjällkartor Sarek and Padjelanta

SALTOLUOKTA FJÄLLSTATION (400M)

Established in 1912, the attractive and charming wooden buildings of the *fjällstation* occupy a large clearing in the birch forest 150m from the ferry landing jetty. From the main building there are grand views westwards out across Langas Lake to the distant mountains of Stora Sjöfallets. Saltoluokta is located beyond the reach of roads and is only linked to the outside world via the ferry back across to Kebnats, and for this reason the site has an atmosphere of undisturbed charm.

Facilities are excellent and include a well-stocked shop, free Wi-Fi for guests, *bastu*, restaurant, 100 beds, electricity and payphone. Camping is SEK100 for STF members with pitches located in the trees west and downslope of the buildings; take care choosing your pitch as some can be prone to ant infestation. Campers have use of the excellent *servishus* which includes *bastu*, showers, drying room and a large kitchen. Weather forecasts as well as timetables for the Langas crossing and 93 bus are posted on noticeboards.

The restaurant is very popular and advance booking is recommended (call from Vakkotavare or book on arrival at the *fjällstation*). The all-you-can-eat breakfast (0700–0900) is SEK95 and highly recommended as a start to a day's walking. Saltoluokta is a Bussgods agent and parcels will be held at a cost of SEK50 per week.

Start	Saltoluokta STF Fjällstation 400m
Finish	Sitojaure STF Fjällstuga 640m
Distance	19.3km
Ascent	425m
Descent	185m
Grade	Moderate
Time	6hr 30min
Terrain	Lakeside to lakeside via open fell, some mixed birch and coniferous forest
Shelter	Emergency shelter at Avtsusjvágge
Camping	Wild – many opportunities for wild camping above the treeline although some stretches have no water close by. Those wishing to wild camp at the end of the day will have to do so some 3km before reaching Sitojaure or walk a further 3km having made the lake crossing. Paid – Sitojaure STF Fjällstuga
Resupply	Basic supplies from private boat operator in Sitojaure

This is a day of big landscapes and fabulous views, the best being back northwards over the shoulder during the climb onto the high fell. This is the longest stage for a week or more and even those who took the opportunity to fully rest at Saltoluokta may be feeling the distance by the day's end. There are some stretches on the high fell where water is scarce, so care will be needed to avoid running out. Those wishing to cross Sitojaure as well today should aim to get there before the last motorised service at 1700. However, be aware that decent camp spots are nearly an hour's walk onward after the crossing.

Pick up the sign for Sitojaure outside the reception of the fjällstation and follow the sandy trail into the mixed forest of birch and conifers. ▸ Ascend, gently at first then more steeply as the trail passes the first of two 'Ravinen' (gorge) signs. At the second such sign the birch begins

The conifers soon diminish although lingon and bilberry are plentiful.

131

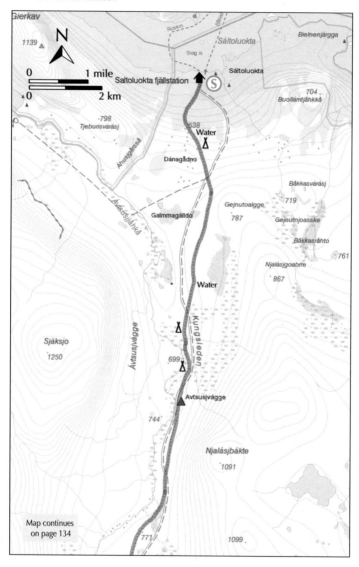

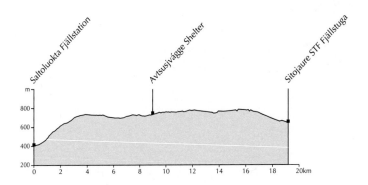

to thin, allowing spectacular views to open up behind you; endless blue lakes, steep dark cliffs, green fell and snowy mountains fill the northwest quadrant. Having emerged from the treeline, these views just get better and better as height is gained, more than fair compensation for the effort involved. Lulep Gierkav (1059m) dominates the scene with its steep black cliffs and mighty sweeping talus.

Continue climbing for 15min above the treeline to a stream with willow and birch trees nearby, this will be the last opportunity to replenish water for the next 4km; good camp spots can be found nearby. Resume the steady ascent and soon the long escarpment of **Sjäksjo** (1250m) will come into view; this extensive feature will accompany you for much of the day during the 12km traverse of the **Ávtsusjvágge Valley**. The slope relents at around 720m and this is a good opportunity to rest and savour the superlative views to the north and contemplate the Ávtsusjvágge that lies ahead to the south.

Continue easily along the trail, noting three buildings 500m downslope to the west on the plain of the Ávtsusjjåhka River, from this point onwards regular streams and water will once again be encountered on the trail. Continue in easy ascent, passing through the occasional willow thicket to reach the **Avtsusjvágge shelter**

133

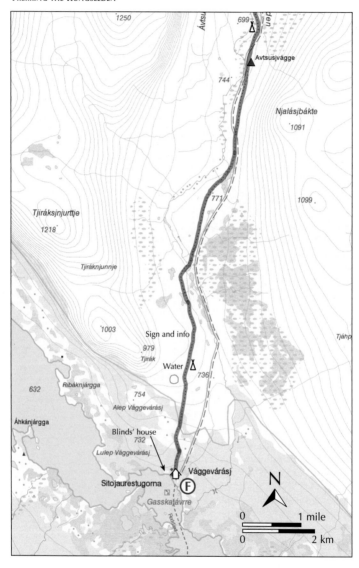

which is about half way to Sitojaure and an excellent place for lunch.

The Ávtsusjvágge Valley

> The Avtsusjvágge shelter (720m) – the shelter is perfectly positioned 9km from Saltoluokta and 11km from Sitojaure. The main building is of a wooden *prisma* construction with a metal roof. Water can be sourced 200m to the west. Outside, a south facing bench will allow you to soak up the sun and views on a fine day, while the simple interior offers a table, a sleeping bench and a wood stove. A latrine and woodshed complete the facilities. Although information with regards to the upcoming lake crossing at Sitojaure might be expected in the shelter, unfortunately, this is not the case.

Leave the shelter and continue along the Ávtsusjvágge in gradual ascent, passing two small lakes after 4km; the

Information is
also posted here
concerning the
upcoming crossing
of the interconnected
Gasskajávrre and
Gåbddåjávrre Lakes
between Sitojaure
and Svijnne.

Ávtsusjjåhkå, elevated on the opposite western hillside, is now hidden from view. Passing a third small lake soon after the first pair marks the end of the long, gentle ascent from the shelter. Descend and take planks across the Ávtsusjjåhkå which has reappeared once again, slow-moving and close to its source, as witnessed by the pools and marsh grasses all around. Ascending gently one final time, pass a lake that is spanner-shaped on the map and, 1km further on, reach the apex of the climb where there is a **sign** for Ribákluokta and Vággevárásj, the latter being the Sámi village close to Sitojaure STF Fjällstuga. ◀

Descend from the sign and cross the broad open fell, beyond which forest and lakes will be seen for count-less kilometres. Soon the last good water source until Gasskajávrre Lake is passed. Those wishing to wild camp are advised to pitch here due to the lack of water until the lake shore, where there are few camp spots other than those at the STF *fjällstuga* where payment is required. Follow the trail into the birch forest all the way to the STF *fjällstuga* (**Sitojaurestugorna**) which sits immediately on the lakeside. ◀ Keep an eye out in the latter stages for a sign indicating a trail off to the right and the **home of Lars and Anna Blind** who operate the motorised boat crossing and also offer other supplies to walkers. Those continuing directly to the STF fjällstuga will arrive there five minutes after passing the Blinds' sign.

In the forest you
will enter the
Ultevis Fjällurskogs
Nature Reserve.

SITOJAURE STF FJÄLLSTUGA (640M)

Sitojaure STF Fjällstuga offers basic services that includes beds for 18 in a single cabin with a dedicated room for dog owners; all those staying on site share the facilities of this cabin. Camping is on a small grassed area some 50m east of the *stugvärd*'s cabin; the camping area, like the rest of the site is very prone to insects in season. There is no shop or *bastu* on site. Cards can be used for payment as can Euros and Norwegian Krone. Weather forecasts are available from the *stugvärdar* and those with mobile phones can access the Telia network.

STAGE 10
Sitojaure to Aktse

Start	Sitojaure STF Fjällstuga 640m
Finish	Aktse STF Fjällstuga 570m
Distance	8.3km walking (plus 3.6km boat crossing)
Ascent	325m
Descent	395m
Grade	Easy
Time	3hr 20min (walking)
Terrain	Lake crossing, open fell and birch forest
Shelter	Emergency shelter at Svijnne
Camping	Wild – camp spots close to the treeline at the start and finish of the day. No water sources on the open fell to support camping. Paid – Aktse STF Fjällstuga
Resupply	Well-stocked shop at Aktse STF Fjällstuga

This relatively short day traverses forest and open fell and also includes the steepest, although short-lived, section of ascent on the Kungsleden. Camp spots are numerous up on the open fell, although the lack of water renders them unusable to all but those willing to carry additional supplies. The descent to Aktse at the day's end reveals magnificent views of the colourful Lájtávrre delta overlooked by the vertical face of Skierffe. Those planning to continue on beyond Aktse today should note that the final motorised service is at 1700 and that once across, there are no good camp spots for nearly 8km. If this is too far, a very poor spot can be found within the forest after 5km. Many walkers spend an additional day at Aktse in order to make the walk to Skierffe's summit and back, a very worthwhile and spectacular detour.

After Teusajaure and Langas, the Sitojaure Lake crossing is the third mandatory boat crossing you have to negotiate on the southward journey along the Kungsleden. Although STF-provided rowing boats are available to make the 3.6km journey across to Svijnne, walkers

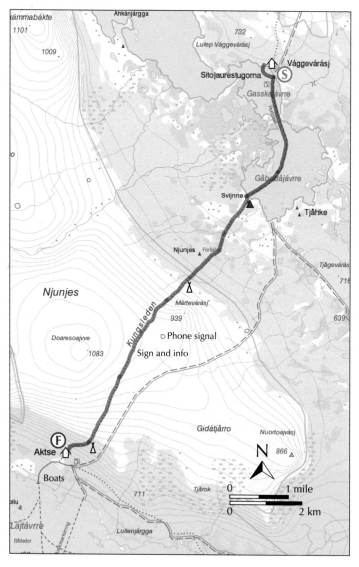

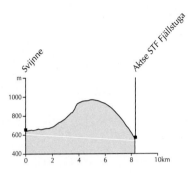

should not underestimate the undertaking for a number of reasons. Firstly, if you are obliged to make three crossings to return a boat, the 11km of rowing required is likely to take up a very large part of both your walking day and your energy! That said, the onward walk to Aktse is relatively short and if you don't have to return a boat the row and walk are comfortably combined in a day.

Arriving at Sitojaure after the long row from Svijnne

A second consideration is that the route across the lake follows a definite course that must be accurately followed. This course (marked by wands sticking out of the water) avoids the shallows. Straying from the course will inevitably lead to grounding. Thirdly, Sitojaure and Svijnne are not in line of sight of each other and you must be certain of the route before setting out. Finally, the crossing is open to the elements and some rowers get blown off course by the wind, necessitating rescue by the Blinds' power boat. These winds can quickly whip up strong waves in the shallow waters which some may find uncomfortable and intimidating. You are strongly advised, therefore, to seek the advice of the *stugvärdar* and the Blinds prior to making a rowed crossing. For those electing to row, the boats are located on the shore adjacent to the camping area.

The motorised crossing is privately operated by the helpful and knowledgeable Lars and Anna Blind who live by the lakeshore 350m west of the *fjällstuga*. Their house can be reached via a very rocky trail from the *fjällstuga* or directly from the Kungsleden as indicated by the sign passed 5min before arrival at the *fjällstuga*. The Blinds also operate a kiosk at their house selling dried reindeer meat, fresh fish (when available), home-baked bread, beer, soft drinks and chocolates. Walkers are welcome to call by, purchase a drink and relax as they wait for the next crossing.

The 20min crossing costs SEK300 (SEK150 for under-13s) each way and departs from the Blinds' house at 0900 and 1700 daily, calling at the STF *fjällstuga* en route. Departures from Svijnne are at 0930, 1230 and 1730 daily. Those catching the service from Svijnne must phone ahead to book on 073 0799603 or 010 4016347. It is important to book ahead as the boat will not automatically come across if there are no passengers from Sitojaure. For those travelling northwards and wishing to cross from Svijnne, information on where a phone signal is available is included in the description for Stage 10. Additional crossings to those scheduled can be negotiated with the Blinds.

From Svijnne's jetty pick up the trail and head into the birch forest where almost immediately you will find a small basic shelter. Inside there are benches and a table, although no woodstove; information for the lake crossing to Sitojaure is posted inside the shelter. Nearby is a small building for rubbish. There is no latrine on site nor is the immediate area suitable for camping. Follow the well-marked trail into the forest crossing a bridge after 1km and reach the treeline after a further 1.5km. ▶

Good camp spots can be found just above the treeline and water sourced from the stream 200m to the northwest, the last opportunity to do so for 5km. Continue onto the open fell, climbing more steeply as height is gained. Follow the trail across a very steep and rocky section of trail northwest of **Mártevárásj** that is in places somewhat loose. This is the steepest climb of any on the Kungsleden. The steepness soon relents at a brow into a gradual climb to the broad saddle to the east of **Doaresoajvve** (1083m). A small sign indicates that it is possible to call ahead to the Blinds and book a crossing from Svijnne back north to Sitojaure (tel 073 0799603). It

Views ahead are of the low domed peak of Mártevárásj (939m).

Lájtávrre

is also possible to get a phone signal from the area of the circular reindeer enclosure.

Follow the well-marked trail across the saddle and very soon begin descending across a boulder-littered hillside and into a sublime landscape. The dark cliffs of Tjahkelij (1214m) will loom into view on the far south side of the subtly and multi-hued Lájtávrre delta. Skierffe (1179m) remains tantalisingly hidden, although eventually its unmistakable chisel-shaped profile will emerge above the near hillside off to the west. Proceed slowly towards the treeline as once inside, much of this stunning vista will be lost to sight.

Immediately on reaching the treeline note the **sign** and trail that head off northwestwards to Skierffe, a 7km walk away. For Aktse, follow the sometimes rocky and steeply descending trail into the mixed birch and conifer forest and 10min later, pass a camp spot and stream, the first reliable water in 5km. Continue your descent to a clearing and the perfectly situated Aktse STF Fjällstuga. ◄

Twenty minutes into the next stage, you will encounter the next mandatory boat crossing – a 3km journey across Lájtávrre Lake: the motorised service operates at 0900 and 1700, or you can use the STF rowing boats.

> Literally meaning nine, the name **Aktse** refers to a large boulder on the hillside where reputedly, nine bears were slain. Originally, the Sámi had *kåtor* at Aktse as the reindeer migrated through the Rapadalen Valley. Settlers came in the 1830s and through hard work and determination, cut and cleared trees to produce the hay meadows that are still present to this day. The Swedish Nature Conservancy (Naturskyddsföreningen) who have a cabin on the meadows, keep the haymaking tradition alive at Aktse by organising an annual harvest weekend every July.

Aktse's hay meadows with Skierffe on the right

AKTSE STF FJÄLLSTUGA (570M)

Located in the Rapadalen Valley and sitting in a clearing on the forest edge, Aktse commands views over nearby grass meadows and the Lájtávrre beyond, a truly stunning location where one could spend a couple of days relaxing and exploring Skierffe. The *fjällstuga* has beds for 34 split between two cabins. Campers pitch in the nearby meadow and share the facilities of the more downslope cabin, while dog owners have a dedicated room in the upper cabin. There is a *bastu* and a well-stocked shop where you can pay using bank cards as well as Norwegian Krone and Euros. Weather forecasts and information regarding the upcoming lake crossing are available on site. Although idyllic, Aktse does have a reputation for having lots of insects.

In the meadow below the STF *fjällstuga* stands another much smaller cabin replete with a magnificent set of moose horns set on the gable end. This building belongs to the Svenska Naturskyddsföreningen. Formerly it was possible to stay here having obtained the key from the STF *stugvärdar*. Unfortunately, this is no longer the case and those wishing to stay at the Svenska Naturskyddsföreningen cabin should make arrangements with the organisation directly.

STAGE 11
Aktse to Pårte

Start	Aktse STF Fjällstuga 570m
Finish	Pårte STF Fjällstuga 500m
Distance	19.1km walking (plus 3km boat crossing)
Ascent	420m
Descent	490m
Grade	Moderate
Time	6hr 50min (walking)
Terrain	Lake crossing, open fell and large stretches of forest
Shelter	Emergency shelter on south shore of Lájtávrre. Emergency shelter at Jågge
Camping	Wild – very limited for the first 7km within the forest. Some good spots on the open fell and once again, limited within the forest for the final 5km. Paid – Pårte STF Fjällstuga
Resupply	Nil

This relatively long stage spends much time within forest and only 7km of the stage is spent on the open fell. Consequently the day can seem to drag on and if the insects are out, the forest sections can become somewhat tiresome. There are great rewards to be had on the walk to Pårte, not least of which are the elevated views down into the verdant Rittak Valley with its rich multi-coloured wetlands. Pårte STF Fjällstuga feels very remote in its forested seclusion.

DOGS

Dog owners planning on walking to Skierffe should note that the peak lies within the Sarek National Park where dogs are not permitted. Leashed dogs are only permitted in the park (all year round) if they are on the Kungsleden itself, Skierffe is 7km off the trail and therefore out of bounds.

Pick up the trail downhill from Aktse and continue on through the pretty grass meadows below. As you walk you will be looking westwards into the Rapadalen Valley with fantastic views of Skierffe's vertical cliff, flat-topped Nammásj (823m) and the snowy mountains of Sarek in the far distance. Continue on boardwalks the entire way through birch forest and down to the shoreline, allow 20min from the *fjällstuga*. Whatever means is used to cross the lake, motorised or rowing, the views remain superlative throughout.

The 3km crossing of the Lájtávrre takes 15min using the motorised service, considerably longer by STF rowing boat. The motorised service departs Aktse at 0900 and 1700 daily, returning directly at 0915 and 1715. At the time of writing the service is jointly provided by the STF some days and by a private operator on others. The crossing costs SEK200 (SEK100 for under-16s) each way and can be paid by cash or card for the STF service, cash only for the private service. If electing to use the STF rowing boats, the considerations are similar to those for the previous crossing at Sitojaure. Unlike at Sitojaure however, shallow waters and grounding are not an issue. The crossing is straight and direct with the occasional small orange buoy to mark the line. The motorised service and STF

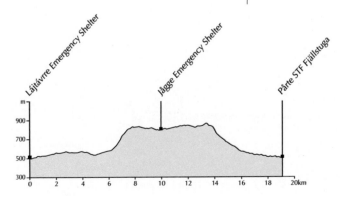

145

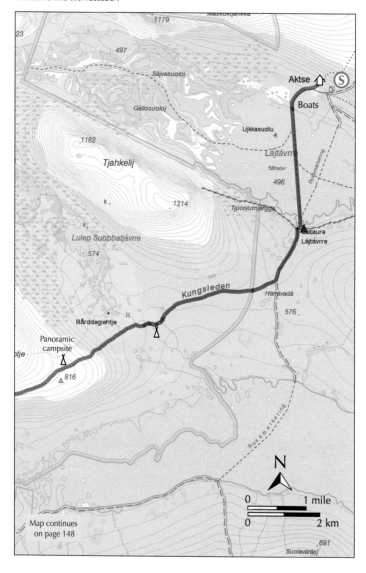

rowing boats are 20min walk away from the STF *fjällstuga* at Aktse.

If rowing across Lájtávrre, put ashore by the jetty in the sheltered cove that also contains a boathouse. Pick up the well-marked trail which immediately passes an emergency shelter before passing through a **reindeer fence** and on into the mixed birch and coniferous forest.

> The emergency shelter – of the by now familiar wooden construction with a metal roof – has benches and a table inside but no woodstove. A latrine can be found the other side of the reindeer fence as can a small building for rubbish. There is room for camping around the shelter.

Follow the compacted trail in a gentle climb through the forest and after 2km enter the Sarek National Park. Continue for a further 3km to a wooden bridge that crosses the Suobbatjåhkå River. A small camp spot will be found on the west side of the bridge.

> Founded in 1909 and containing 200 peaks over 1800m, **Sarek National Park** is the most mountainous area in Sweden and also receives the most rainfall. The park is largely devoid of marked trails, huts and bridges, making it a popular destination for the well-equipped and experienced walker and mountaineer.

Continue for 5min and cross a second larger bridge at which point the conifers end, leaving solely birch forest. Climb gently for 20min and more steeply again as the trail makes for the trecline at 800m and the open fell above, some 7km of walking from the shoreline.

Follow the trail onto the open fell, climbing more gently once above the trees. Once free of the forest's confines, the unobstructed fellside offers wonderful views in all directions; Tjaktjajávrre reservoir sweeping from southwest to southeast, the mountains of Sarek to

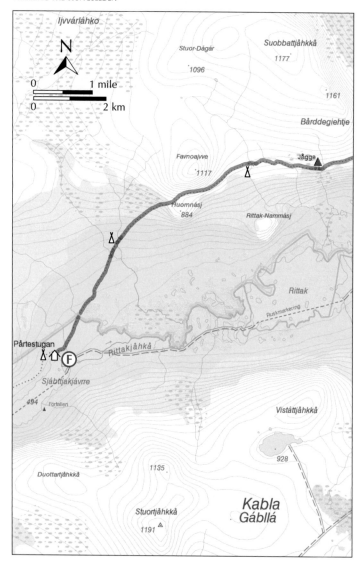

Evening colour above Lulep Suobbatjávrre

the northwest and the serene lake-filled valley between Tjahkelij (1214m) and Suobbattjåhkkå (1177m). ▸ A little higher on the fell, pass an area that has many camp spots with views that are hard to better, water can be sourced from a stream 300m to the north. Continue ascending until, some 30min above the treeline, a brow is reached on the southeast flank of **Bårddegiehtje**. Follow the now very gently descending trail that skirts the hillside parallel to the otherworldly Rittak Valley for 2km. Re-enter the birch treeline to reach the **Jågge** shelter.

The valley is an offshoot of the Rapadalen and is favoured by moose and bear.

Jågge shelter (800m) – the shelter is basic and sits in a small clearing in the birch forest. It is made of wood with a felted roof, an older design than that commonly seen on the trail. The rather dark interior consists of benches, a table and a wood stove, while outside a latrine and rubbish storage complete the itinerary. Although Jågge's clearing is small, there is room to pitch a couple of tents within it. Water is sourced from the nearby stream.

Climb gently away from Jågge through the birch until, 15min later, the open fell is once again reached and then traversed to the Jåkkejågåsi River which is crossed by a high metal bridge whose height is testament to just how high the waters rise during the spring thaw, good camp spots can be found on the west bank. Continue comfortably along the undulating trail which squeezes between the treeline and the steep south face of **Favnoajvve** (1117m) and then descends to take the pass between Favnoajvve and **Huomnásj** (884m). Once through the pass, begin descending more steeply for 5min and then back into the birch treeline where the trail is rocky at first. Descend onwards and into mixed forest, cross two bridges in short succession, the first being wooden with a camp spot nearby and the second being metal. Now in more gentle descent, traverse a number of very boggy areas as well as small ridgelines for 2km to a final wooden bridge that marks the boundary of the Sarek National Park. Continue for one last easy kilometre to Pårte STF Fjällstuga (**Pårtestugan**). Information on the crossing to Aktse for those walking northwards is posted on a sign just before arrival at the *fjällstuga*.

PÅRTE STF FJÄLLSTUGA (500M)

This quiet *fjällstuga* is located in the trees on a small peninsula that sticks out into Sjábttjakjávrre Lake and this combination of forest and lake make for a site that is unsurprisingly, very insect prone. The *fjällstuga* has beds for 26 spread between the *stugvärd*'s cabin and a cabin close by. Camp spots are found close to the buildings and facilities are shared with those in the cabin. There is neither a shop nor *bastu* on site and no facility to pay using bank cards; Euro and Norwegian Krone are accepted. Weather forecasts are available and the notice boards in the buildings have excellent information such as meal timings at Kvikkjokk *fjällstation* and information on the motorised service between Svijnne and Sitojaure. A spot for those wishing to camp close to the *fjällstuga* but not pay is located 5min along the trail in the direction of Kvikkjokk.

STAGE 12
Pårte to Kvikkjokk

Start	Pårte STF Fjällstuga 500m
Finish	Kvikkjokk STF Fjällstation 330m
Distance	15.2km
Ascent	90m
Descent	260m
Grade	Moderate
Time	5hr 20min
Terrain	Forest throughout
Shelter	Nil
Camping	Wild – limited spots within the forest. Free – Kvikkjokk STF Fjällstation
Resupply	Well-stocked shop at Kvikkjokk STF Fjällstation

This stage is spent wholly within ancient coniferous and birch forest which can at times feel somewhat claustrophobic, especially if there are grey skies and rain. It will not be a day of grand views but it does represent an opportunity to reflect. The gradients are never too taxing, although the going underfoot can be uneven and break the walking rhythm. Kvikkjokk Fjällstation represents an opportunity to re-stock, recharge and for those going no further, depart the trail. Day walkers from Kvikkjokk are a common sight during the day.

Retrace the trail that came into Pårte and pick up the sign and trail for Kvikkjokk. 5min after the sign, a small camp spot will be passed. The trail undulates through mixed birch and conifer with plentiful cloudberry by the wayside. Underfoot, tree roots and rocks become more common and serve to slow the pace. Take a small metal bridge across the Tjoaltajåhkå River which has a small camp spot on its west bank. Continue following the good paint markers for 2km and cross through **two reindeer fences** in short succession. ▶ Follow the very uneven and

Views will now open up out and across Stuor Dáhtá Lake to distant snowy peaks.

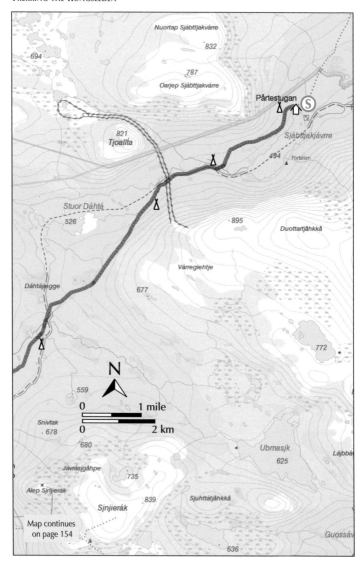

Map continues
on page 154

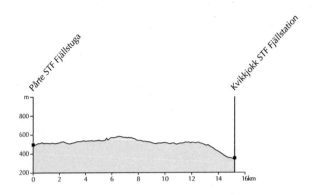

tiring trail along the lakeshore for 1km passing a number of camp spots on the way.

Back in the forest, ascend the trail tediously over rocks and roots, only where the trail levels out does the going ease with boardwalks and fewer rocks underfoot. Descend gently to a small clearing where information

View over Stuor Dáhtá Lake

153

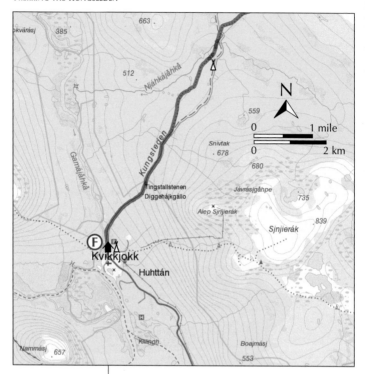

The next section/ stage begins with a mandatory boat crossing, operated by Björn Sarstad and Helena Adolffson. Contact them on 070 2053193 or 073 8006232 to pre-book – or they can sometimes be found enjoying a drink in the fjällstation lounge.

boards and signs indicate 7km to Kvikkjokk. Very soon, cross a low wooden bridge and 300m further on, a larger high-sided wooden bridge which has camp spots on its south side in the trees. Continue easily on the level then on an extended although gentle ascent, the last of the day. Walk on the level again for 1km before beginning the final descent of the day. The going now is good and the gradient never too steep. On the way down, pass a large overhanging boulder (**Tingstallstenen**) which marks the final 30min of walking. Pass through a barrier accompanied by the roar of the **Gamájåhkå River** and follow the trail for the final kilometre to the fjällstation at **Kvikkjokk**. ◄

The fjällstation's shop is the only one in Kvikkjokk

KVIKKJOKK STF FJÄLLSTATION (330M)

Kvikkjokk *fjällstation* represents the lowest altitude on the Kungsleden. It is located at a roadhead besides the roaring rapids of the Gamájåhkå and is part of a wider although small community; most of Kvikkjokk's residents are seasonal, with only four living there all year round. The *fjällstation* today serves all functions in Kvikkjokk; shop, bar and place to eat, there are no other facilities in this small hamlet.

The *fjällstation* is smaller and more compact than those of Abisko and Saltoluokta and some of the facilities are beginning to tire and show their age. The station has bed capacity for around 60 and a large grassy clearing for campers. Camping is free, but a service charge is payable for use of the other facilities on site such as the communal cooking and washing areas.

The shop, now the only one in Kvikkjokk, is well-stocked for walkers' needs. Bank cards can be used, as can Euros and Norwegian Krone. It is also possible to obtain cash at the reception counter using your bank cards; guests can obtain up to SEK500 at no cost while non-guests can obtain the same amount at a charge of SEK5 per SEK100.The *bastu* is small, lacking in charm and only available to those who are sleeping in the *fjällstation*. Weather forecasts are available as are bus timetables (service numbers 44,

155

Kvikkjokk STF Fjällstation

43, 93 and 47) for those departing the trail via Jokkmokk; train timetables (Tågkompaniet Norrtåg Train) for onward travel from Jokkmokk are also available. It is possible to travel to Jokkmokk, spend four hours there and get back to Kvikkjokk all in a single day if you set off on the 0900 bus, return time to Kvikkjokk being 1810. Information is also posted and available for boat crossings to the north (Aktse and Sitojaure) and to the south; the immediately upcoming boat crossing of Sakkat Lake and that across Riebnes Lake in three days' time (Jan and Eva Johansson, tel 073 0358673 or 070 6968045, eva@vuonatjviken.com).

There is mobile phone reception at the *fjällstation* and Wi-Fi costs SEK15 for 100Mb, SEK50 for 500Mb. The communal lounge in reception is convivial and a good place to meet other walkers. Walkers can post parcels ahead to Kvikkjokk where they are held securely by the STF staff.

SECTION 3 –
KVIKKJOKK TO
JÄKKVIK

Cloudberries at Gistojávrátj Lake (Stage 14)

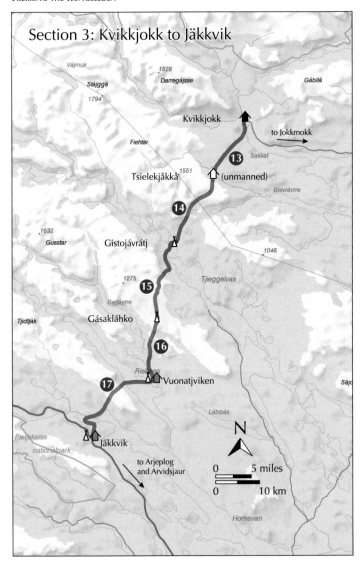

Section 3: Kvikkjokk to Jäkkvik

SECTION 3
Kvikkjokk to Jäkkvik

Start	Kvikkjokk
Finish	Jäkkvik
Distance	87.6km (walking distance 78.5km)
Ascent	1805m
Descent	1695m
Terrain	Forest predominating over fell
High point	Southeast flank of Jåhkågaskatjårro 1000m (Stage 15)
Boat crossings	Mandatory: Sakkat, Riebnes and Harrselet-Hárresavvun (9.1km). Note that the Harrselet-Hárresavvun crossing on Stage 17 is the only boat crossing on the Kungsleden without a motorised service: the 400m must be rowed.

This is the least popular section on the Kungsleden, essentially for practical reasons. There are no STF *fjällstugor* to support the less experienced walker or those who do not wish to camp and carry a heavy pack. Access at each end of the section is neither easy nor efficient and there are three boat crossings to make, one of which must be rowed. This stretch also has a somewhat unjust reputation for being uninspiring compared to other sections. Little surprise then that your days walking between Kvikkjokk and Jäkkvik are likely to be ones of undisturbed solitude; maybe this is exactly what you came for anyway!

Though food and a sleeping bag are necessary, it is possible to complete this section without a tent if two successive days are walked as follows; between Tsielekjåhkå and the *kåta* on stage 15 (29km) and between the *kåta* and Vuonatjviken (20km) where there is accommodation readily available.

For those who cherish remote areas and being away from it all, this section will not be a disappointment. Most of the forest encountered is birch and therefore sparse, light and unoppressive in nature. Out on the open fell,

During Stage 16 the Arctic Circle will be crossed, though the spot is unmarked on the ground.

walkers will find unrestricted views in all directions and the ability to make camp at will. ◄

Access

Kvikkjokk sits at a remote roadhead linked by the 47 bus to Jokkmokk. Jokkmokk can be reached by 44 bus from Gällivare or alternatively, the 43 bus serves Jokkmokk from Murjek, which is on the SJ train network.

Jäkkvik, like Kvikkjokk, is a remote community where transport in and out requires care and forward planning. The (weekday only) 104 bus links Jäkkvik with Arjeplog which in turn is linked by onward bus (26 or 17) to Arvidsjaur from where direct Nordica flights can be taken to Stockholm. Arvidsjaur is not on the SJ rail network and an onward 26 bus or Tågkompaniet Norrtåg train will be required to link into that network at Jörn.

Maps
- 1:75,000 Outdoorkartan Blad 4 (Kvikkjokk-Jäkkvik) OR
- 1:100,000 Fjällkartan BD14 (Kvikkjokk-Jäkkvik) OR
- 1:100,000 Calazo Fjällkartor Kvikkjokk, Ammarnäs and Arjeplog

STAGE 13
Kvikkjokk to Tsielekjåkkå

Start	Kvikkjokk STF Fjällstation 330m
Finish	Tsielekjåkkå 620m
Distance	11.9km walking (plus 2.7km boat crossing)
Ascent	480m
Descent	190m
Grade	Moderate
Time	4hr 30min (walking)
Terrain	Lake crossing, dense mixed forest and airy birch forest
Shelter	Emergency shelter at Mallenjarka
Camping	Wild – a number of spots in the sparser birch forest.
Other accommodation	Small unmanned STF *fjällstuga* at Tsielekjåkkå
Resupply	Nil

Although this stage is spent wholly within forest, the majority of the walking is through sparse and airy birch which lifts the spirits. The trail is good throughout and any steep climbs are relatively short-lived. Tsielekjåkkå is a picturesque riverside location and a joy to camp at, insects permitting!

Pick up the road heading southwards from the fjällstation. Follow the road round a leftwards bend and then immediately take a turn-off on the right which leads (passing a water well) down to the lakeshore from where Björn and Helena's boat will depart.

There are no STF-provided rowing boats to make this crossing and walkers must make use of the private motorised service operated by Björn Sarstad and Helena Adolffson, permanent residents of Kvikkjokk. They can be contacted on 070 2053193 or 073 8006232 or even better, found in the lounge at the fjällstation having a beer. The crossing costs SEK200 with under-12s going free, payment is cash only. There is no set timetable as all crossings are by prior arrangement. Quite often but not

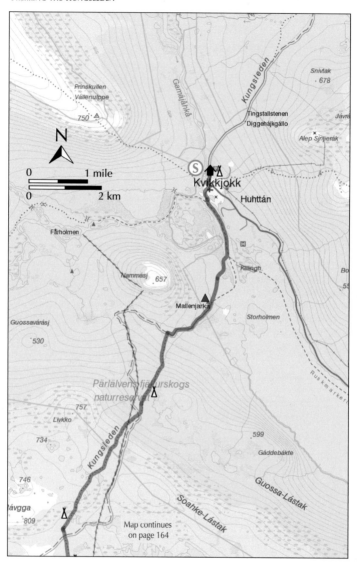

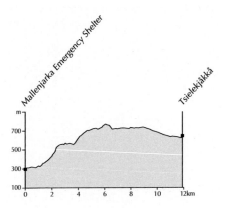

always either Björn or Helena will call at the *fjällstation* to fetch those booked onto the service. The 2.7km crossing takes 20min and weaves its way through tree-lined channels across to the south shore of Sakkat Lake where a long wooden jetty awaits.

From the jetty, follow the well-marked trail for 100m into the mixed coniferous and birch forest to pass a neat emergency shelter at **Mallenjarka**.

The Mallenjarka shelter (330m) – is of the normal wooden construction with a metal roof. Inside it is fresh and clean with benches and a table; there is no wood stove. There is a restricted-use mobile phone which allows walkers wanting to cross to Kvikkjokk to contact Björn or Helena. Information concerning the motorised service is posted on the outside of the shelter under the small eaves. Outside there is a latrine and a bin for rubbish. There is little space for camping besides the shelter.

Continue on the flat for 1km before beginning to climb, gently at first then giving way to a steeper and stonier path. Continue more strenuously to where a small

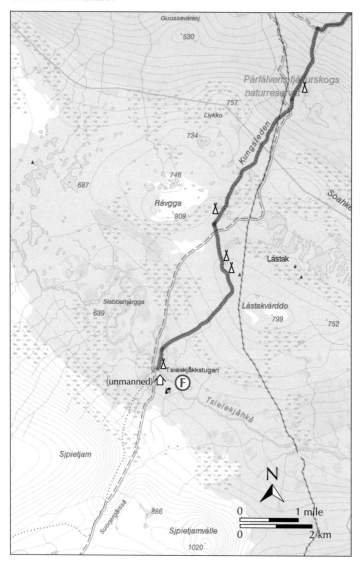

waterfall cascades; cross the stream where logs are piled up. ▸ Once across the stream continue steeply again for 20min and until level with a small knoll to the northwest, after which the path levels out and descends to a stream where there is a poor camp spot. Continue along the undulating trail before climbing steeply once again. Pass through an old wooden **reindeer fence** beyond which the conifers end, leaving solely birch forest to walk through. ▸ Continue as the ascent eases, passing two small lakes and at a third, views ahead open up of a carpet of forest for many kilometres. Descend briefly crossing a stream and then gently ascending, pass a cluster of small lakes where poor camp spots can be found. Continue on beyond the lakes and make a distinct swing to the left. Continue ascending slowly for 1.5km up the broad, gentle and open northwest ridge of **Lástakvárddo** (799m). Pass small lakes on the way up where decent camp spots can be found.

Descend gently from the ridge noting and smelling the numerous juniper bushes as you go. Still descending, the open spaces within the forest become more numerous

Keep an eye open for termite mounds on the ascent.

The birch forest is less humid and much less claustrophobic in its atmosphere.

Typical mixed forest en route to Tsielekjåkkå

and larger and the appearance of boardwalks and a small lake herald the final kilometre of walking to Tsielekjåkkå. A metal suspension bridge crosses the wide **Tsielekjåhkå River** to where a wooden fjällstuga (**Tsielekjåkkstugan**) stands elevated on the south bank.

TSIELEKJÅKKÅ FJÄLLSTUGA (620M)

The small *fjällstuga* is metal roofed and owned by the STF. The interior is basic and equipped with two wooden benches for sleeping, a small table, wood stove and a *hjälptelefon*. Information on the motorised crossing to Kvikkjokk is available for those walking northwards. Payment is required for use of the *fjällstuga* and this can be made either at the next manned STF facility (Kvikkjokk STF Fjällstation if travelling northwards, Aigert STF Fjällstuga if travelling southwards) or by giro payment for which instructions are provided. Overnight fees are SEK100 for STF members and SEK150 for non-members, under-16s stay for free if they are members, SEK50 if non-

The fjällstuga *at Tsielekjåkkå*

members. All day visitors, member or not, pay SEK40. There is no rubbish disposal facility on site and although there are an axe and saw, there is neither wood nor woodshed provided! A small *prisma* latrine stands nearby. Numerous good camp spots can be found on both sides of the river, although the north bank has the better and more sheltered spots. The entire site is prone to insects including the *fjällstuga*'s interior which is badly infested in season, meaning it is better to camp!

STAGE 14
Tsielekjåkkå to Gistojávrátj

Start	Tsielekjåkkå 620m
Finish	Gistojávrátj 510m
Distance	17.6km
Ascent	330m
Descent	440m
Grade	Moderate
Time	6hr
Terrain	Open fell followed by airy birch forest
Shelter	Nil
Camping	Wild – many opportunities, mostly on the open fell
Resupply	Nil

Much of this moderately long stage is spent on the wide open fell, a welcome change following two days spent within the forest. Although the panoramas are of low-lying landscapes and rounded fells, they are no less wonderful to the eye.

Depart Tsielekjåkkå gently ascending through fast-thinning birch trees; after 1km the open fell is reached. Continue an easy ascent across marshy ground that crosses the sweeping foot of **Sjpietjam** and into the beautiful u-shaped valley that is **Suoŋergårsså**. ▶ Follow the trail into the valley to where good camp spots are found besides a simple metal bridge. Ascend more steeply once over the bridge, taking care to cross to the south (left) bank of the stream. Pick up **winter markers** for the rest of this short ascent to the head of the Suoŋergårsså which here, forms a very shallow ravine. Nearing the top of the ravine bear right and away from the winter markers which continue in a southwesterly direction to Parka. Continue gently ascending to where the ground levels out to reveal impressive views across the open fell to Goabddábákte (1266m), its south face rocky and steep. There are some

Take a final look back north across the vast birch forests on crossing into Suoŋergårsså.

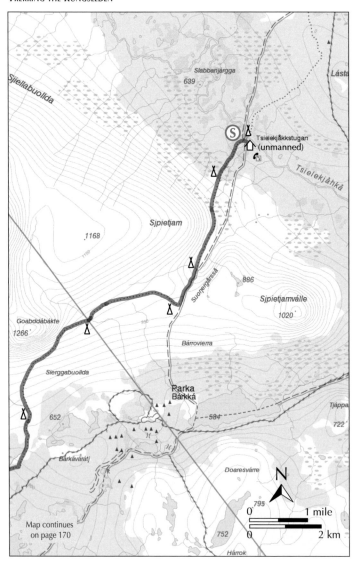

camp spots here although the location is exposed. Pick up the **painted pole markers** and make very good time on the easy ascent across 3km of open fell.

At the apex of the long ascent, cross a small metal bridge (with very good camp spots nearby) and begin descending to cut right beneath the dark and impressive

Goabddábákte

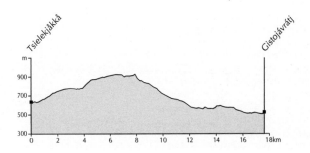

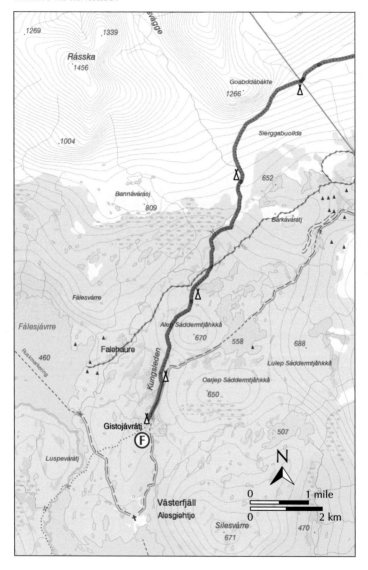

cliffs of Goabddábákte. At the foot of the rock face is a moraine ridge, descend off this steeply at first then more gently across the open and boulder-strewn slope of **Sierggabuollda**. The descent is comfortable and affords the opportunity to take in the forest and fell that stretch for many kilometres to the south. Merge with the east bank of the noisy Fálesjåhkå River and continue descending, passing many good potential camp spots. ▶ Now enter the treeline and diverge from the river bank for a short period. Soon, after again re-joining the river bank, a bridge across to the west bank will be seen although not taken. Leaving the river behind for a second and final time, traverse a clearing that contains abundant lingon and cloudberry before entering a very dense section of birch. Cross a **reindeer fence** and climb away to very soon arrive at a lake with spots to camp. Continue on the trail, taking in a couple of short sharp ascents as the west flank of **Alep Sáddermtjåhkkå** (670m) is traversed. Continue descending through mixed forest and cross a stream with camp spots. Follow a boardwalk along the edge of a clearing to arrive 15min later at **Gistojávrátj Lake**.

Perfectly rounded alluvial rocks will be seen besides the path on this section.

Gistojávrátj (510m) – this lake is surrounded by birch forest and the best camp spots are to be found on arrival, spots are small and need careful selection to avoid tree roots and rocks. Exploration of the general area will uncover plentiful supplies of cloudberry in season. The combination of water and trees makes for a very insect-prone camp spot and for this reason, many walkers continue south to camp on the open fell many kilometres away, southwest of the Pite River.

STAGE 15
Gistojávrátj to Gásakláhko

Start	Gistojávrátj 510m
Finish	Gásakláhko 900m
Distance	19.7km
Ascent	540m
Descent	150m
Grade	Challenging
Time	6hr 40min
Terrain	Birch forest initially then open fell with boulder plateau
Shelter	*Kåta* on open fell
Camping	Wild – very limited in the forest, many more options on the open fell
Resupply	Nil

Midway between Kvikkjokk and Jäkkvik, halfway along the Kungsleden, this stage feels and indeed is, remote. Once across the Piteälven gorge the going is somewhat demanding for a few muddy kilometres, although you can take cheer in the knowledge that the open fell awaits. Above the treeline a remarkable boulder-strewn plateau is traversed before a final long easy climb and descent across the expansive fell. Phone signal will be available towards the day's end which will allow you to make arrangements for the future Riebnes Lake crossing at Vuonatjviken.

Depart Gistojávrátj, descending gently towards the Pite River whose mighty roar can be heard from a long way off. The trail is rocky in places although never too taxing.

> The **Pite** flows southwards from Fálesjávrre Lake into Tjieggelvas Lake via a wide channel that narrows at its southern extreme to form a ravine through which the waters are squeezed. The area is popular with fishermen and they may be encountered once the river is reached.

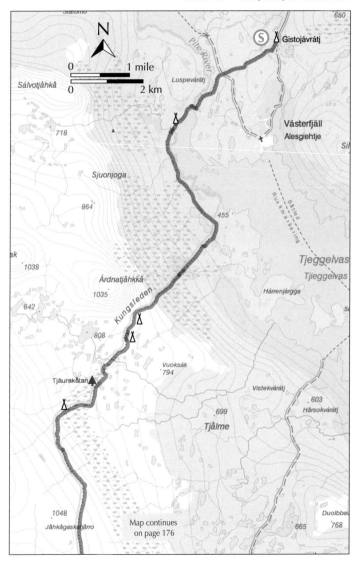

Map continues
on page 176

173

The view while crossing the Pite River

On reaching the bank of the **Pite**, stay parallel with it southwards for 1km, much of the time on boardwalks. On reaching a latrine and metal suspension bridge, take the bridge across the ravine via a small rocky island and a second identical bridge to the far bank.

Once across the Pite but still within forest, continue awkwardly over some rocky steps and a very muddy trail that winds parallel to the river. Pass a small wooden boathouse and arrive at good riverside camp spot furnished

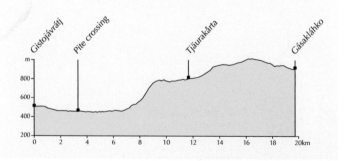

with a latrine, benches and rubbish bin. Continue a little easier now over a slight rise and take two simple metal bridges across the Sálvojåhkå River. Continue on the level but still very muddy trail. Pass Tjålmukjávrátja Lake that occupies a clearing, bear right as signposted at the lake's southern tip and begin ascending once the forest is re-entered. Climb fairly steeply on a sometimes muddy trail to a brief easing in the angle, cross a wooden bridge and then begin climbing more steeply once again for the final 20min to the treeline, this section being thankfully drier underfoot. ▶

As the trees thin the views expand considerably giving fantastic vistas across Tjieggelvas to the east.

Now on the open fell, continue an ascent which soon eases as it makes for the brow just below the (1035m) steep and grassy south flank of **Árdnatjåhkkå**. Crest the brow to reveal low and open rolling fell. Continue 500m further on and crest a second much lower brow that reveals a large boulder-strewn plateau dotted with small lakes. Traverse this plateau for 3km, initially crossing four wooden bridges and three simple metal bridges in due course, all of which have good camp spots nearby. The well-marked trail gently weaves, dips and climbs its way through this rocky landscape, although the going is never too arduous.

Kåta (790m) – the trail directly passes a traditional wood and turf *kåta* (Tjäurakåtan) with a small lake nearby. The interior has a soil floor that is clean and dry. This would make for a good shelter, especially

The kåta is largely weatherproof and provides the only shelter on Stage 15

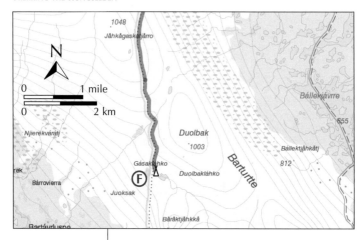

in an emergency, and there is room for four to sleep comfortably, more at a squeeze. As is traditional, the roof apex has gaps to allow wood smoke to vent from inside.

From the **kåta** climb steadily straight up onto the fell to ever-expanding views. Cross a small metal bridge with good camp spots and then swing left to cut diagonally up the broad open slope; apart from a brief initial steep section that is marshy, this climb is kind and pleasurable in the main. Level out close to a small lake and a bit further on, enjoy the new views ahead that include Riebnes Lake, the next boat crossing. Telephone signal will appear at the small lake, allowing the Riebnes crossing to be arranged. Descend easily for 3km to the lake at **Gásakláhko** crossing a very shallow valley en route.

Gásakláhko (900m) – this pretty lake sits in a shallow basin and affords only limited protection, camping can be found anywhere in the area. Reindeer are common visitors and the views southwards are rich and varied. Collect drinking water from the outflow on the east side of the lake.

STAGE 16
Gásaklåhko to Vuonatjviken

Start	Gásaklåhko 900m
Finish	Vuonatjviken 520m
Distance	12.9km
Ascent	20m
Descent	400m
Grade	Easy
Time	4hr 40min
Terrain	Open fell then birch forest
Shelter	Nil
Camping	Wild – very limited throughout. Free – Vuonatjviken.
Other accommodation	Self-catering accommodation available at Vuonatjviken
Resupply	Some limited (and surprising) opportunities at Vuonatjviken

On this stage you cross the Arctic Circle – although this milestone is strangely not acknowledged or marked. Magnificent views accompany the initial descent off the open fell into the birch forest where the going throughout is steady and never difficult. Vuonatjviken is a community of surprises, opportunities and the point of departure for the next lake crossing. Be sure to phone ahead while the signal is still strong on the open fell.

Pick up the trail in easy descent from Gásaklåhko passing **Båråktjåhkkå** (953m) and enjoying the vast views across lakes and forest, snowy peaks will also be seen in the far distance to the west. Cross boardwalks and enter the birch forest. Continue and cross a wooden bridge sat in a clearing – somewhere south of which, the **Arctic Circle** passes through. ▶

Continue easily through the forest passing a long lake to the west of the trail. Pass a second body of water which is in fact an inlet of Gåbdåkjávrre Lake which in turn, forms part of a deltaic system linking Bartávrre and Riebnes Lakes. Follow the trail as it heads along

There is no sign to mark the point where you leave the Arctic Circle and by the time two lakes straddling the trail are reached, you will have passed it.

177

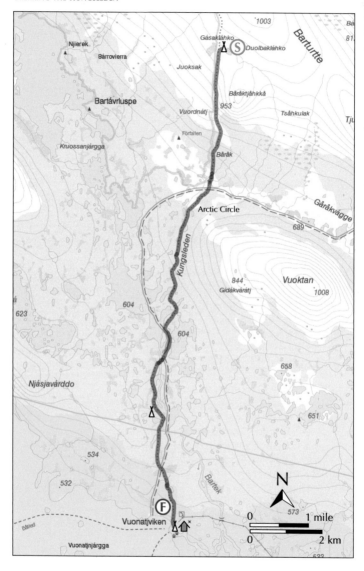

a peninsula to reach at its tip, a raised boardwalk that crosses open water to another peninsula. Traverse this second peninsula and take a metal suspension bridge that spans the frothing waters of the **Bartek River** to arrive at the west bank of the deltaic system.

Follow the undulating trail, which is marshy in places, to cross a wooden bridge; there is a poor camp spot on scruffy bare earth. Continue easily through the forest for 3km to the hamlet of **Vuonatjviken**. ▶

The next stage begins with a mandatory boat crossing, operated by Jan Johansson: it is essential to pre-book (tel 073 0358673, 070 6968045 or eva@vuonatjviken. com – or call in to Jan's office).

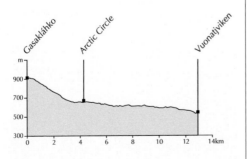

179

Vuonatjviken, a place of surprises

The small lakeside community of **Vuonatjviken** (520m) is permanent home to the Johansson family (Jan and Eva) whose Sámi forbearer, Abram Johansson, first settled the site in the late 19th century. Today a dozen buildings occupy the hamlet, most being given over to tourism, fishing and holiday rental.

Camping is free at Vuonatjviken and the pitches are located down by the water. A latrine is provided for campers. Self-catering accommodation is available for groups of up to 10 people. A guideline price is SEK850 per night for three sharing. Surprisingly, Vuonatjviken also has a restaurant, although this requires booking at least a day in advance. Otherwise, trust to luck and hope that you arrive when another party has booked and the restaurant is open.

Those holidaying at Vuonatjviken kindly offer services to walkers so don't be surprised if you are invited in for a meal or to take a shower (all for free) as you wait for the crossing.

Jan Johansson's office (100m from the lake's edge) also has a small store offering basic supplies such as cold drinks, ice cream, eggs and snacks. Meals can also be bought from the Johanssons and the *halstra* (fish barbecue or broiler) outside their office is as good a place as any to enjoy any food you've purchased. The Johanssons are very helpful and will do their best to provide what you want if they have it in stock or in their house.

Many aim to arrive at Vuonatjviken in the afternoon and cross the Riebnes the same day. Once across there are no immediate camp spots and a 3km ascent is required to reach the open fell and the first suitable camp spots. This may influence your decision whether or not to camp at Vuonatjviken or push on.

STAGE 17
Vuonatjviken to Jäkkvik

Start	Vuonatjviken 520m
Finish	Jäkkvik 440m
Distance	16.4km walking (plus 6km and 0.4km boat crossings)
Ascent	435m
Descent	515m
Grade	Moderate
Time	5hr 40min walking
Terrain	Lake, much forest and some open fell
Shelter	Open-sided shelter at rowed crossing (Tårvekallegiehtje)
Camping	Wild – some on the open fell, very limited within the forest. Paid – hostel in Jäkkvik.
Other accommodation	Hostel and self-catering at Jäkkvik
Resupply	Comprehensive and very well-stocked shop in Jäkkvik

Once across Riebnes Lake, it's a reasonable climb and a fairly long day's walk into Jäkkvik, largely through forest. In the latter stages of the day the final boat crossing on the Kungsleden is made, a straightforward 400m row. Jäkkvik has charm aplenty and much to recommend it as a place to re-stock and rest.

Riebnes Lake crossing – Jan Johansson (tel 073 0358673 or 070 6968045, eva@vuonatjviken.com) operates the motorised service across Riebnes Lake and his office is 100m from the lake's edge, the office is marked 'reception'. The 6km crossing, the most expensive and complained about on the Kungsleden, costs SEK350 each way and can be paid for using cash or card. Crossings do not run to schedule and are not necessarily daily. Therefore, make sure you arrange in advance otherwise you may be cooling your impatient heels in Vuonatjviken for a day or more waiting for the next service. There are no STF rowing boats at Vuonatjviken nor any other providers for the Riebnes crossing.

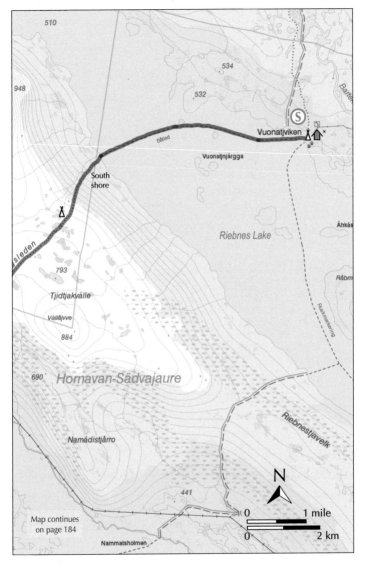

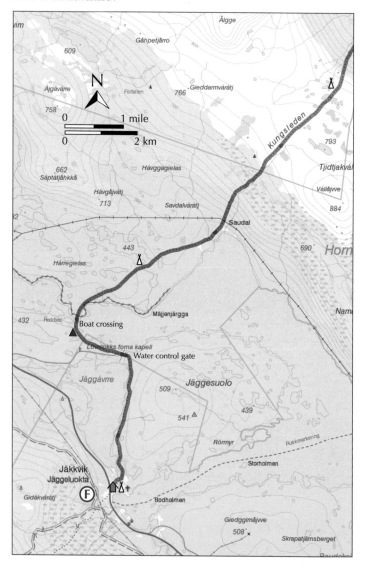

The lake crossing from Vuonatjviken takes 20min and delivers you to a rocky beach on the south shore where there is a latrine and a small cluster of buildings. Follow the Jäkkvik sign into the birch forest and begin what soon becomes a steep ascent with minor marshy sections. Follow the **faint paint markers** for 2km to the treeline and open fell. Continue more easily past some small lakes with camp spots, an hour's walk from the shoreline. Traverse the fell easily and quickly before descending

Twisted tree trunk at Saudal

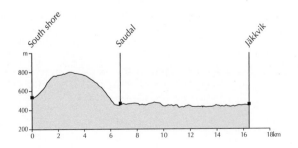

185

Curlews can be seen and heard out on the open fell.

back into the forest. ◄ Continue downwards over a sometimes rocky and muddy trail to **Saudal** where conifers begin to appear among the birch.

A long undulating section now ensues. Begin by following the trail briefly through a powerline clearing then back into the mixed forest. Do not follow any white trail markers in this area. The trail is marshy in many places although not rocky and a reasonable pace can be maintained. After a couple of kilometres, pass two lakes in quick succession, navigating a tricky rock step. Cross a metal bridge with potential camping nearby and continue onwards through the forest. Pass through a **reindeer fence** and 15min later, arrive at the shore of Tjårvekallegiehtje Lake where STF rowing boats await.

Tjårvekallegiehtje Lake crossing, the final mandatory crossing on the Kungsleden (and the only one without a motorised service), negotiates a 400m-wide channel linking Tjårvekallegiehtje and Harrselet Hárresavvun lakes. The crossing is straightforward and the line obvious although prone to a current that will try to push the boat eastwards. The south shore has an open-sided wooden shelter (440m) which makes for a good aiming mark when rowing.

Once across, continue from the shelter through forest for 500m and emerge onto a gravel track. Turn left onto the track and follow it eastwards for nearly 1km to where a large **water control gate** is located. Cross the gate and veer immediately rightwards onto a path through the trees. Do not go straight onwards having crossed the gate, a mistake that is easily made if unaware. Continue through the trees and emerge besides the shores of **Jäggávrre Lake**, Jäkkvik will be seen in the distance at the lake's far end. Follow the easy path along the lakeside for the final 3km into **Jäkkvik**.

JÄKKVIK (440M)

The Kungsleden passes through the very centre of this extremely attractive and tranquil village which sits on the 95 road linking Norway with Arjeplog to the east. Although a seemingly sizeable village, there are only around 20 permanent residents in Jäkkvik, the rest being seasonal and holiday visitors. Fortunately, Jäkkvik is not prone to insects and locals remark how low the numbers have fallen in recent times. For walkers there are two main facilities that will provide for all your needs, the Kyrkans Fjällgård hostel and the Handlar'n shop at the petrol station. Jäkkvik is also an exit and entry point for the Kungsleden although public transport is very limited; the local 104 bus to Arjeplog leaves the petrol station at 1105 on weekdays only, travel time to Arjeplog is just over an hour. The Silverexpressen 200 service which ran almost daily ceased in 2013. The mobile network reception in Jäkkvik is good.

Handlar'n shop
The Handlar'n shop seems to fulfil almost every commercial function in Jäkkvik. Summer opening hours are 0900–1900 Monday to Thursday, 0900–2000 Friday, 0900–1800 Saturday and 1000–1900 Sunday. Cards can be used for payment and although there is no ATM, no-limit cashback is available at a three per cent surcharge. Walkers can also obtain the key for the upcoming *stuga* at Pieljekaise for SEK150 at the shop. Handlar'n also serves as a Bussgods agent for the receiving and sending of parcels. The shop is extremely well-stocked with every imaginable conventional food type, fresh and packaged, plus a limited supply of dehydrated trekking food. Gas, batteries, petrol, toiletries and meths are also available, deliveries to the shop are made every Wednesday. If you need anything while in Jäkkvik speak to Anna in the Handlar'n – she is extremely helpful and has a wealth of knowledge (tel 0961 21050 or www.jackvikfjallcenter.com then click on the Handlar'n logo (Swedish only) and www.facebook.com/handlarnjackvik).

Kyrkans Fjällgård hostel
Kyrkans Fjällgård doubles as the local church and an independent hostel although neither function overtly intrudes upon the other. The hostel is extremely friendly as well as being spacious, clean and well equipped throughout. The hostel is not manned round the clock, although clear instructions are posted by the entrance for arriving walkers. Facilities include a kitchen and dining room, lounge, outdoor seating area, showers, *bastu*,

The friendly and spacious Kyrkans Fjällgård

washing machine and driers; there is no Wi-Fi in the hostel. Dogs are permitted in the annexes although not the main building. Camping is available on the lawns around the hostel and campers have the use of a dedicated service room that contains kitchen, showers and toilets. The hostel has a capacity of 80 which includes rooms within the main building and satellite self-catering annexes. Bed prices are SEK250 for an adult, SEK100 for under-18s. Camping is SEK70 with a variety of charges for other services that include *bastu* SEK60, washing machine and drier SEK50 apiece, towel hire SEK60. Bank cards are accepted. Canoes can also be hired at the hostel for use on the nearby waters (tel 073 5210369, kyrkans.fjallgard@telia.com, www.kyrkansfjallgardjakkvik.com – Swedish only).

SECTION 4 –
JÄKKVIK TO AMMARNÄS

Moonlit view southwards from Tjiegnatisjávrrie (Stage 20)

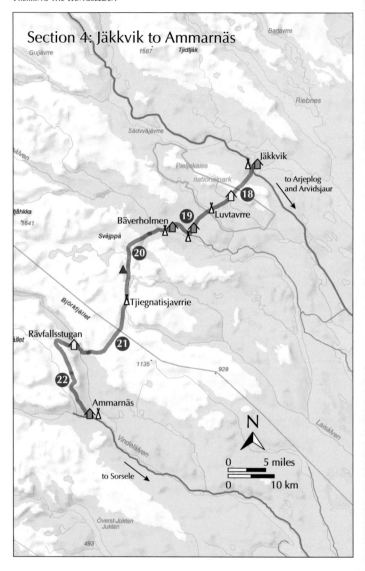

Section 4: Jäkkvik to Ammarnäs

SECTION 4
Jäkkvik to Ammarnäs

Start	Jäkkvik
Finish	Ammarnäs
Distance	91.1km (walking distance 91.1km)
Ascent	1680m
Descent	1700m
Terrain	Mainly forest initially, then mainly open fell thereafter
High point	Northern end of Björkfjället Plateau 940m (Stage 21)
Boat crossings	Optional: Iraft Lake

This is another quiet section although it has a great deal to recommend it in terms of the landscape and the friendly communities encountered along the way. There are also no more mandatory boat crossings. Much of the section's first half is within forest, although being largely birch, the impression is always open and bright. The trail passes through Adolfsström and Bäverholmen, both of which offer an opportunity for accommodation, the former for resupply as well. Beyond Bäverholmen you will climb onto and traverse part of the Arjeplog Fells, an area much prized for its fishing. ▶ The section is easily completed without a tent as in addition to the facilities at Adolfsström and Bäverholmen, there are non-STF *stugor* at Pieljekaise and Rävfalls and an overnight shelter at Snjulttjie. For those with a tent, the possibilities for camping and dividing up this section are endless.

This area is popular with wildlife enthusiasts and time spent engaging with them and the fishermen is well spent.

Many walkers make use of a shortcut to Ammarnäs that cuts out the Rävfallsstugan and the following day's final stage. This is not, as some would believe, the line of the Kungsleden. Those intent on completing the entire trail should continue to Rävfallsstugan – which is a wonderful experience in itself – and complete the walk to Ammarnäs from there over the high open fell. Ammarnäs has a range of facilities for walkers and also some fascinating landmarks that are very much worth a visit.

Access

Jäkkvik is a remote community where transport in and out requires care and forward planning. The transport hub for Jäkkvik is Arvidsjaur, which is served by direct Nordica flights from Stockholm. Arvidsjaur is not on the SJ rail network: a 26 bus or Tågkompaniet Norrtåg would be required to connect with the SJ network at Jörn. The 26 and 17 bus services link Arvidsjaur with Arjeplog from where the (week-day only) 104 bus serves Jäkkvik.

Ammarnäs lies at a road head and is linked to the outside world by the 341 bus service to Sorsele (70min). From Sorsele, buses 36 and 31 take you to Umeå whilst the 45 bus will take you to Arvidsjaur.

Maps

- 1:75,000 Outdoorkartan Blad 5 (Jäkkvik-Ammarnäs) OR
- 1:100,000 Fjällkartan BD16 (Vuoggatjålme-Ammarnäs) OR
- 1:100,000 Calazo Fjällkartor Kvikkjokk, Ammarnäs and Arjeplog

UNMANNED STUGA KEYS

Only enough *stuga* keys are in circulation for the number of people that can be accommodated in the respective *stuga*. Keys for any particular *stuga* are issued from at least two locations, as walkers travelling in either direction will have need of them. Therefore, at any one time, there are *stuga* keys waiting to be issued in at least two locations; keys that have been issued and are with walkers; and finally, keys that have been used and are being returned to their point of issue in a pre-paid envelope (issued with the keys) to be issued once again. The dynamics and possibilities when it comes to working out availability is therefore mind-boggling and extremely difficult. For these reasons, it is not always possible to pre-book *stuga* keys.

STAGE 18
Jäkkvik to Luvtávrre

Start	Jäkkvik 440m
Finish	Luvtávrre 600m
Distance	13.2km
Ascent	450m
Descent	290m
Grade	Moderate
Time	4hr 45min
Terrain	Mainly forest, some open fell
Shelter	Allmän Raststuga and Pieljekaisestugan
Camping	Wild – some on the open fell, very limited within the forest
Resupply	Nil

This pleasant stage involves a transit of Pieljekaise National Park, an unspoiled area of undulating low fell and subalpine birch forest. Although the park is home to moose, lynx, bear and wolverine, all are very wary of people and you are extremely unlikely to encounter any of them. The Allmän Raststuga is a delight while the Pieljekaise *stuga* offers an overnight alternative for those who collected the key beforehand. The stage ends at the southern boundary of the national park where camp spots can be found at Luvtávrre. Many walkers will make the journey from Jäkkvik to Adolfsström in a single day.

Resume the marked trail southwards out of Jäkkvik, crossing the main 95 road and following a gravel road uphill for 400m to the Ljungpiparvágen street sign. From here the trail is signposted into the birch forest. Ascend through the forest, passing but not crossing a bridge. Very soon a second bridge appears, cross this and continue more steeply although still comfortably. ▶

Continue ascending and at the treeline, **take great care where the trail divides**. Confusingly, red paint markers are seen on both branches where the trail splits. The

Many flowers as well as ferns and low-lying arctic bramble line the trail.

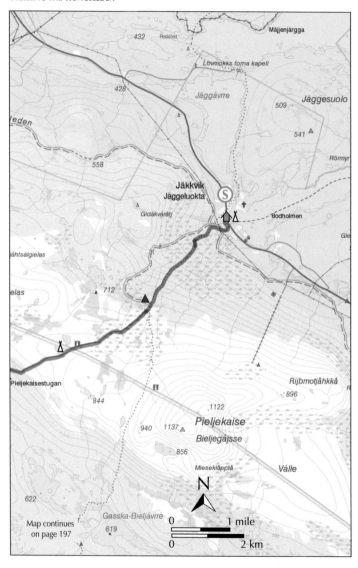

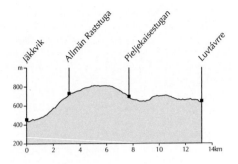

right-hand branch leads within 50m to the wonderfully situated Allmän Raststuga which is well worth a visit.

Allmän Raststuga (710m) – this clean and tidy cabin is generously provided by the local council and features an outdoor picnic area and a spacious main building with tables, benches, a wood burner, gas stoves and even a solar powered heater. Behind the main building are two latrines and a wood store. Sleeping in the cabin is not permitted except in an emergency, although there are small tent pitches in the immediate vicinity and a stream for water 100m to the northwest.

Airy birch forest leads out from Jäkkvik

195

Back at the trail divide, follow the branch that continues straight ahead and 10m further on arrives at an unambiguous sign. Continue gentle ascending onto the open fell. Level out on the broad plateau west of **Pieljekaise** (1122m) and besides a small lake with an **information board** marking the boundary of Pieljekaise National Park.

Pieljekaise National Park, one of the smallest and least known in Sweden, was founded in 1909 largely to protect the birch forest, which is today very much unspoiled. Although it's unlikely you will encounter large species in the park, it is worth keeping a keen eye open for traces such as droppings, tree rubbing and footprints.

Continue past a lake lying 300m within the park boundary where good camp spots are to be found with extensive views in all directions. Begin descending (to picturesque views) into the very heart of the park's birch forest; the entire vista is one of contrasts, open fell, birch forest and snowy peaks in the far distance. Follow the trail into the treeline and 15min later, arrive at the Pieljekaise fjällstuga (**Pieljekaisestugan**) hidden among the trees.

PIELJEKAISE FJÄLLSTUGA (700M)

The *fjällstuga* is provided by the local council and consists of two wooden buildings which occupy a very confined site within the birch forest. The ground is generally uneven and dense with foliage so there are no suitable camp spots in the vicinity; this may be just as well given the voracity of the local mosquito population. The buildings are left unlocked, although you will need a key to access the small four-bed dormitory in the main building. The communal area is dominated by a fine set of moose horns and provided with a wood stove, tables, benches, a two-ring gas burner, cutlery and crockery. A porch precedes entry allowing (most) insects to be kept at bay. The dormitory has a table and bench with two double bunks equipped with mattresses only. The second building houses the wood store, spare bottles for the gas burner and the rubbish. Close by are a pair of latrines and a spring from where you may draw water.

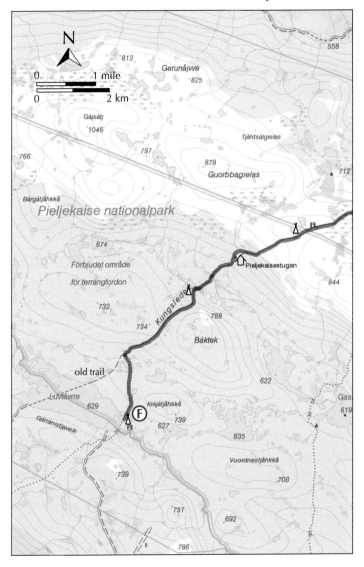

Most walkers pick up the *fjällstuga* key on chance in Jäkkvik although it can be pre-booked. Reservation and collection, depending on the direction of travel, is via the Handlar'n in Jäkkvik or the Handelsbod shop in Adolfsström, at a cost of SEK150 per night. The key should be returned using the pre-paid envelope provided when it is collected.

Here the foliage seems to press in, creating an impression – albeit temporary – that borders on the claustrophobic.

Descend from Pieljekaise where the going is now rockier. ◄ Continue descending for 2km and cross a wooden bridge on a valley floor, small restricted camp spots can be found close by. South of the bridge, climb a short steep section that heralds the start of the ascent from the valley via the flanks of **Báktek** (788m). Continue for 2km to a small wooden sign and make a swing to the left; a rerouting of the old trail which descends for 30min until **Luvtávrre Lake** is reached.

Luvtávrre (600m) – this quiet and peaceful lake was formerly taken by rowing boat until the trail was recently rerouted. The first camp spots encountered on arrival are at lake level, dry and insect-free given any slight breeze. A little further along the shore the ground rises and elevated spots can be found among the trees.

View across Luvtávrre

STAGE 19

Luvtávrre to Bäverholmen

Start	Luvtávrre 600m
Finish	Bäverholmen 460m
Distance	14.4km
Ascent	120m
Descent	260m
Grade	Easy
Time	5hr
Terrain	Forest with town midway
Shelter	Nil
Camping	Wild – very limited. Paid – Adolfsström and Bäverholmen.
Other accommodation	Self-catering in Adolfsström and Bäverholmen
Resupply	Well-stocked shop in Adolfsström. Restaurant in Bäverholmen

An easy day's walking through light airy forests, some by the lake. Midway the trail passes through Adolfsström which offers the opportunity to shop, eat cake and take an optional motorised ride to Bäverholmen – maybe one for those who've eaten too much cake. Bäverholmen is a tiny and picturesque riverside community with a friendly *värdshus* serving up moose and reindeer steaks. Those hoping to sleep in the Rävfallsstugan in the near future should collect a key in Adolfsström as they pass through.

Pick up the trail along the southeast shore of Luvtávrre and cross a left-curving wooden bridge that marks the southern boundary of the Pieljekaise National Park. Ascend the hillside steadily on a good dry trail and after 2km, begin the descent toward Adolfsström. Continue to signposts and a forest track which is followed across a wide wooden bridge with simple bench seating nearby. Continue along the forest track ignoring any offshoot trails, even the ones that are confusingly marked with red paint. On reaching a track junction, bear left and

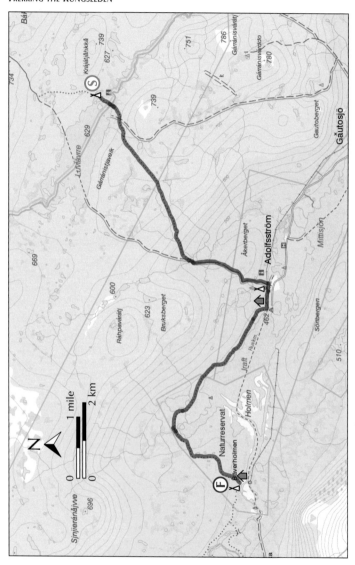

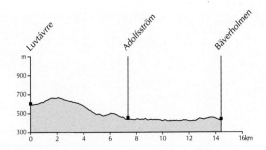

continue to reach the main tarmacked road that runs through **Adolfsström**. Bear right along this road to stay on the Kungsleden and pass all the main facilities.

ADOLFSSTRÖM

The village developed from around 1770 onwards in response to a growing lead and silver mining industry. Today tourism and fishing are the lifeblood and most services are orientated in these directions. Adolfsström's permanent residents total 25 although the size of the village indicates just how many people come into the area in the summer.

On passing through, the first place of interest encountered is Johanssons Fjällstugor which is a multi-functional concern offering self-catering accommodation, camping (SEK55), helicopter services (largely to take fishermen into remote areas) and tourist information. Campers have use of a *servishus* that includes toilets and showers although there are no cooking facilities. There is also a *bastu* costing SEK95 for guests and SEK120 for non-guests. Showers are SEK10. The tourist information is very much orientated towards helicopter services and fishing, and seems somewhat oblivious to the needs of walkers (0961 23040 and info@fjallflygarna.se).

Further along the road is the Handelsbod which is shop, café, accommodation and the source of keys for the *stugor*. Marianne, the owner and a font of all knowledge, founded the shop back in 1977 when there wasn't one at all in the village. Self-catering accommodation costs SEK350 for a two-person cabin (using shared services), SEK960 for a four-person cabin (all services en suite), there is no camping facility. The shop can best be described as an Aladdin's cave – it is filled with wares and decorated right up to and

Inside Handelsbod

across the ceilings. Maps, meths, reindeer jerky, dried ptarmigan, batteries, sweets, food, reading glasses, ice cream, bread, fresh cakes, hot drinks, beer, cold drinks, cheese, milk – whatever you care to think of can all be purchased. Notable exceptions, however, are dehydrated trekking food and gas. Bank cards can be used although Marianne prefers cash if possible. Cashback is not an option. Marianne is also the agent for the Pieljekaisestugan and Rävfallsstugan keys. These and a pre-addressed return envelope are issued for SEK150 per night. The Pieljekaisestugan key (for those heading northwards) can be pre-booked via Marianne (tel 070 6173041, or info@adolfstrom.com; www.adolfstrom.com/eng/engindex.html) while the Rävfallsstugan key (for those heading southwards) is only available on chance. The Rävfallsstugan does have an unlocked communal area with two beds that all can access, procuring a key guarantees a bed and access to the sauna.

Adolfsström has no ATM, no hostel and the restaurant has closed down. All fuel types, Calazo mapping and cold drinks can be purchased at the 'yellow house' which is along the same road but in the opposite direction to Johanssons Fjällstugor and Handelsbod. Many residents will allow you to camp on their property for a modest fee. Adolfsström is at a roadhead with public transport options limited to thrice-weekly local bus to Arjeplog. This service departs Monday, Wednesday and Friday from outside Johanssons Fjällstugor at around 1630 for the 90min journey. There is mobile phone coverage in the town.

Having filled up on cake and coffee at Handelsbod, continue northwestwards through the village to where the road ends and divides. The Iraft ferry is to the left whilst walkers should head right and across a rickety wooden bridge before passing through a reindeer fence into the mixed forest. Continue easily on the well-marked trail parallel and close to **Iraft Lake**. Follow the trail in a similar manner for 3km before it departs the shoreline to track down the strip of land between the Iraft and Bietsek Lake. Swing left and then cross a wooden bridge. Continue easily for the last 2km and emerge onto the attractive meadows at **Bäverholmen**. Here you will be in the tiny **Yrafdeltats Naturreservat**, a mosaic of dry river-banks, lagoons and sedge marshes. Large areas are also covered by osier, which are prized by moose.

Down left towards the water is the departure point for Iraft Ferry, the motorised service to Bäverholmen. There is no schedule and crossings should be pre-booked (tel 0961 23018). The ferry costs SEK300 for over-19s/SEK200 for under-19s (one person travelling), SEK420/SEK280 (two people travelling), SEK460/SEK390 (three people travelling) and SEK600/SEK400 (four people travelling); children under eight travel free.

Airy mixed forest between Adolfsström and Bäverholmen

BÄVERHOLMEN (460M)

Evening idyll in Bäverholmen, the Värdshus *can be seen in the background*

Today there are few signs of beaver in 'beaver home' although local boatmen report increased signs that hopefully herald their return in the near future. Campers can pitch anywhere along the peaceful riverbank which is very insect prone when there is no breeze. Camping costs SEK60 which includes use of the *servishus* attached to the nearby *Värdshus*, showers require an old type SEK5 coin. The *Värdshus* also offers cabin accommodation for SEK250 per night. The restaurant is open 1200–1800 with last orders at 1750. The menu includes moose, reindeer, meatballs and fish. Soft drinks and snacks are also available; cards are accepted for purchases of SEK60 upwards. The *Värdshus* is family run and very friendly, speak to Therese for any local advice or to book a boat to Adolfsström, call 30min before required departure time (tel 0961 23018, 070 2823018, baverholmsvardshus@hotmail.se).

STAGE 20
Bäverholmen to Tjiegnatisjávrrie

Start	Bäverholmen 460m
Finish	Tjiegnatisjávrrie 700m
Distance	20km
Ascent	360m
Descent	120m
Grade	Moderate
Time	6hr 45min
Terrain	Forest initially giving way to open fell interspersed with forest
Shelter	Emergency shelters at Bárasjuhka and Snjulttjie
Camping	Wild – various spots on the open fell
Resupply	Nil

Following two fairly easy days walking in the forest and a dose of civilisation, this longer stage places the walker squarely back onto the remote terrain of the Arjeplog Fells. The area west of Bäverholmen is very popular with fishermen who will be encountered during the first half of the day; they are generally extremely friendly and happy to impart some of their knowledge of the area. If you're considering camping at Snjulttjie be warned that it is an extremely insect-infested spot – it may be better to push on.

Depart Bäverholmen's meadow in a northwesterly direction and continue through mixed forest where the going is easy. A kilometre further, bear left and arrive at the banks of the wide, noisy and frothing Blassaselet River where there is a camp spot complete with benches and a campfire on the east bank. Cross the large metal suspension bridge and continue easily to join the south bank of the smaller but still substantial **Bárasjuhka River**. Follow the river bank passing a good camp spot where a tributary flows in, and arrive at another metal suspension bridge which is taken to the north bank. Climb a

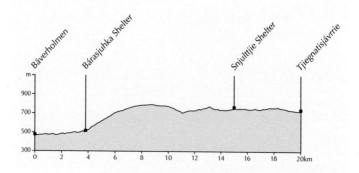

short rise and find, hidden in the trees off to the right, the **Bárasjuhka** emergency shelter.

Crossing the Blassaselet River

Bárasjuhka emergency shelter (490m) – this small attractive log cabin is equipped with benches, chairs and a wood stove with emergency fuel. Outside there is a single latrine, a rubbish bin, a fire area with seating and good spots to camp.

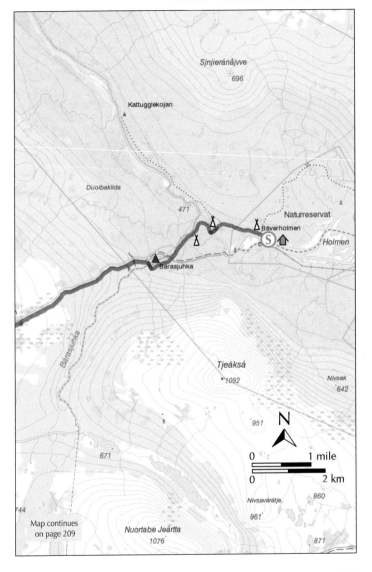

Map continues
on page 209

Continue ascending on what is generally a comfortable ATV track, except for some short steeper sections. ◄ Emerge onto the open fell and continue ascending as before, although now to expanding views. The views to the south are dominated by the bulk and height of Riehkiere (1382m). Continue as the ascent gets ever easier, sometimes crossing boggy sections but never with difficulty. Fishermen may be seen on this section, travelling in both directions; westwards towards Gávasjávvrie Lake in eager anticipation of the fishing ahead and eastwards laden (hopefully) with their catch. Arrive at a set of signposts and bear due south leaving the fishermen to continue westwards, nearby a small lake offers camping opportunities.

Due to the proximity of the mast at Tjeäksá (1092m), the phone signal remains strong until just north of Snjulttjie.

Head southwards from the signposts across easy undulating terrain with many camp spots but no water. Re-enter birch and very soon descend to and take the metal suspension bridge that for the second time today crosses the **Bárasjuhka**. Climb away from the river over sometimes boggy ground and soon level out over undulating terrain with much birch. Pass a lake with good camp spots and ascend, sometimes steeply, the small hill of **Sjkälttjágielas**. Pass Stårbmiejávrrie Lake and 10min later, a signpost for the **Snjulttjie** emergency shelter.

> The Snjulttjie shelter (750m) – (pronounced snul-tyu) is located close to the north shore of Suoluojávvrie Lake, some 400m to the west of the Kungsleden; it is a particularly insect-prone location. The main building is a wooden *prisma* (the original burnt down in 2005) with a simple stark interior comprising narrow sleeping benches, table and a wood stove. Alongside are a twin latrine and a shed for wood storage and rubbish. The best camp spots are closer to the lake besides a large boulder.

Back on the trail, continue southwards to soon emerge from the birch onto level and open heath. ◄ Áhájávrrie Lake will be seen to the southeast along with isolated holiday cabins and buildings. Continue across sometimes

Keep a look out for ptarmigan on the heaths.

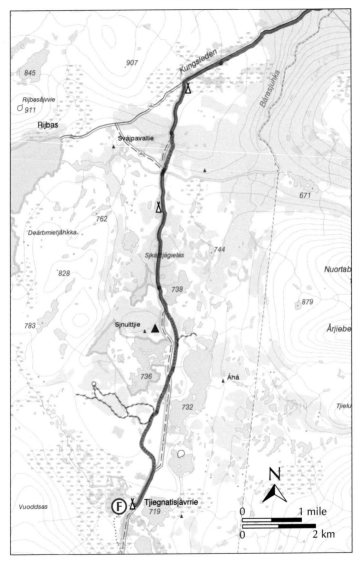

Camping at
Tjiegnatisjávrrie

boggy ground before ascending gently through birch. Traverse a boggy basin with many boardwalks and soon afterwards, swing to the right passing a **reindeer fence**. Continue easily until the trail turns into an ATV track that leads down to a very rusty metal suspension bridge near **Tjiegnatisjávrrie**. Good camp spots abound.

> Tjiegnatisjávrrie (700m) – this idyllic spot stands on the Vuoruojuhka River and commands wonderful views in all directions. Many good, level and dry camp spots can be found in the area. Elevated pitches on the west bank allow you to watch for wildlife from the comfort of your tent.

STAGE 21
Tjiegnatisjávrrie to Rävfalls

Start	Tjiegnatisjávrrie 700m
Finish	Rävfallsstugan 500m
Distance	21.3km
Ascent	260m
Descent	460m
Grade	Moderate
Time	7hr
Terrain	Open fell with forest to finish
Shelter	Nil
Camping	Wild – various spots on the open fell
Resupply	Nil

A long day spent on the fantastically open fell followed by a forested descent into the famous Vindelälven Valley. Rävfallsstugan is perfectly positioned close to a powerful waterfall and is a great place to end the day. Some walkers bypass the *stuga* and shortcut directly to Ammarnäs, effectively cutting out an entire day from the Kungsleden.

Pick up the trail, still an ATV track as it swings and climbs gently to the west in order to avoid marshy ground. Cross boardwalks before diverging leftwards from the ATV track and continue towards the precipice of **Láddievárdduo** (1111m). Cross a boulder-strewn hillock to gain views ahead of a long moraine ridge. Stay parallel with the foot of the moraine on good ground passing a willow thicket and camp spots. Cross a stream that issues from a breach in the moraine and on reaching a second thicket, climb steeply up onto the ridge which is followed to a wooden bridge alongside excellent camp spots. Continue along the ridge, passing numerous camp spots until the ridge becomes indistinct.

Once off the ridge, begin the long pleasant diagonal ascent across the open fell onto the Björkfjället Plateau,

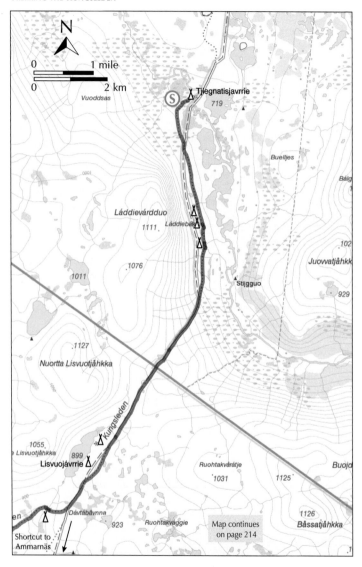

enjoying wide open vistas on the way. The climb steepens towards the end and then relents by a cluster of signposts. The topmost sign indicates that Västerbotten County is now being entered and from here onwards, you should notice that the quality of the boardwalks improves. Continue gently ascending until the trail levels to reveal the plateau stretching off for kilometres into the distance. Push on making excellent time over the unobstructed

The view northwards from the top of the moraine ridge

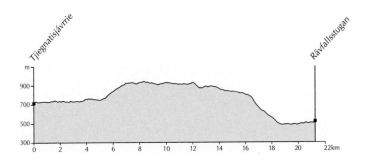

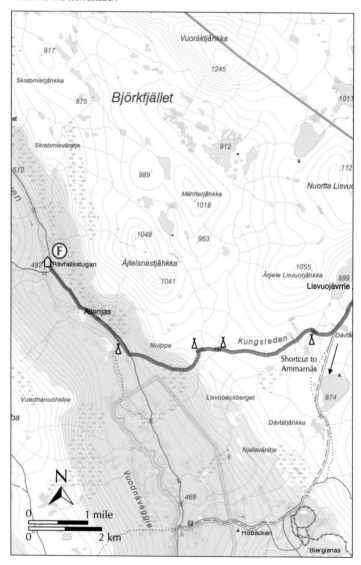

plain. Pass **Lisvuojávrrie Lake** with its numerous camping opportunities and 1km further on, arrive at a wooden signpost. ▶ Swing right and descend along an ATV track to cross a large wooden suspension bridge that has plentiful and excellent camp spots all around it.

Ascend away from the bridge on the ATV track for 500m until a sign directs you across boggy open fell where **the trail is faint, although marked with posts**. Continue level for some time before descending gently towards a large wooden suspension bridge that spans the Guoletsbäcken River. This is the start of the descent into the tree-lined **Vindelälven Valley** whose lower reaches now present a fantastic vista. Continue a short way to a second smaller and simpler bridge; both bridge sites have excellent camp spots. Enter the birch forest and descend more steeply across rocky and boggy ground. Continuing more easily, reach a signpost cluster indicating 3km to Rävfallsstugan.

Follow the trail northwestwards. It turns into a track after 1km. Pass a meadow with a house and barn, there is water to hand and this would make for an excellent camp spot. Pass more meadows and continue to **Aitenjas**

From here it is possible to take an 18km deviation from the Kungsleden direct to Ammarnäs, which will effectively cut a day from the trail.

Meadows and river at Aitenjas

which, with its meadows forms an outdoor museum to pastoral former times. Although there is no permanent community anymore at Aitenjas, locals from lower down the valley still tend the meadows and farm the hay. From Aitenjas, follow the track easily for 2km to the stuga (**Rävfallsstugan**).

RÄVFALLSSTUGAN (500M)

Located in the airy birch forest close to the Rävfalls (fox falls), this wonderful council-owned (unmanned) *stuga* is spacious, comprehensive and well equipped. Many walkers heading into the Vindelälven make use of it both summer and winter. The main cabin has an unlocked communal area with two beds, tables and chairs, a gas stove, wood burner and crockery and pans. Two rooms are locked and only accessible to those who obtained keys. One room contains eight beds, a wood burner and table and chairs, the second room is similar but only has four beds and a wood burner. Mattresses, pillows and blankets are provided for all 14 beds in the building.

Other facilities include a *halstra* with seating, a pair of latrines, a shed for rubbish, *slask* and best of all, right down by the river is a *bastu* that can be accessed by key holders, and from which it is possible to sit and gaze out at the rushing waters. Plentiful wood is stockpiled at the *stuga* for the *bastu* and the wood stoves. The best camp spots on site are found down towards the bridge across the Vindelälven River. A SEK100 charge is levied against all who sleep in the *stuga*. Those who obtained a key will have already paid and information on how other casual users can pay is located in the main cabin. What better than to arrive, stoke up the sauna, have something to eat and then wander down to enjoy the fruits of your fire-lighting labours?

STAGE 22
Rävfalls to Ammarnäs

Start	Rävfallsstugan 500m
Finish	Ammarnäs 420m
Distance	22.2km
Ascent	490m
Descent	570m
Grade	Challenging
Time	7hr 20min
Terrain	Forest to start and finish, otherwise wide open fell
Shelter	Open-sided shelter at Näsbergstj Lake
Camping	Wild – limited opportunities on the exposed fell. Paid – various options in Ammarnäs.
Other accommodation	Wärdshus, hotel and hostel in Ammarnäs
Resupply	Large store and other supplies in Ammarnäs

A day spent climbing onto and then traversing a long and open fell ridge before descending into the resort town of Ammarnäs. As some will have gone direct to the town instead of going via Rävfallsstugan, it is likely to be a day of solitude and reflection. There are no red paint markers on this stage and much reliance is required on winter markers and the use of a map. Some care and attention are required during the final hour of the walk as many confusing trails and paths are encountered close to Ammarnäs. Plenty of opportunities for resupply and accommodation await the weary walker at the day's end.

Cross the impressive wooden suspension bridge to the west side of the Vindelälven and immediately begin the long ascent through the trees to the open fell beyond. The going is good and mostly on ATV track, the gradient is moderate and just within a comfortable range. Skirt a marshy open area emerging into sparse birch, a sure sign that the treeline is fast approaching. On the skyline, Stålluoålggie (1155m) dominates the view ahead, while a glance backwards provides a grandstand view back

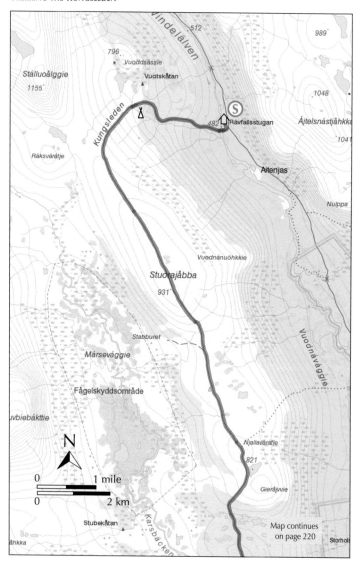

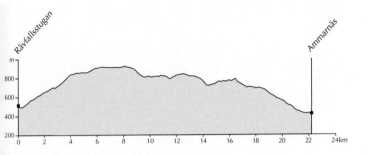

down to the meadows of Aitenjas; to the north the higher reaches of Vindelälven appear forested and dark.

Cross a wooden bridge (camp spots 50m downhill) and continue more steeply over dry ground towards the broad open ridge. Swing left as the angle relents and continue much more easily towards the distant and indistinct summit of Stuorajåbba (931m). Follow the winter markers or alternatively, follow an easier ATV track that parallels them some 50m to the right, being aware that this parallel

Looking back north along the fell ridge towards Stålluoålggie

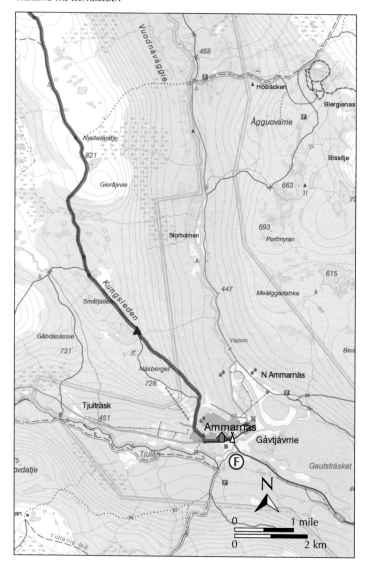

track is indistinct in places. Whichever is followed, all converge at the top of **Stuorajåbba** where a tall pointed cairn marks the summit. ▸

Descend easily, noting the trail snaking away along the ridge for many kilometres ahead. Many lines and trails lead off from the summit so stick with the winter markers initially if the visibility is poor. ▸ The descent is fast and having reached a level area, begin ascending once again to the summit of **Njallavárátje**. Descend to Gieråjvjávrátje Lake and on arriving, swing right. Continue your descent for 10min to a split in the trail. Follow the right-hand branch that has winter markers and continue to the tree-line. Once in the forest continue with more difficulty for some time across rocky and muddy terrain until a rise offers a brief glimpse down to Gautsträsket Lake way down in the valley floor. Descend to Näsbergstj Lake where an open-sided shelter (700m) can be found hidden in the trees 15m to the right of the trail.

Just beyond the shelter, take a left fork and continue through a cutting in the mixed forest, rocky underfoot. Exit the forest briefly before re-entering and merging with other trails and continuing along a wide track. Two minutes later, be sure to bear left just before the forest edge appears and follow winter markers which will lead to a tarmacked road. Turn right onto the road and 200m further on reach a large and busy notice board. Follow the road downhill to a petrol station besides a T-junction. Turn left at this junction and continue for 500m into the centre of **Ammarnäs**.

The ridge is ecologically of poor diversity; very low crowberry, bilberry, dwarf birch and grass.

Ammarnäs is a centre for horse riding and many hoof prints will be seen on the ridge.

AMMARNÄS (420M)

Ammarnäs, the largest habitation encountered on the Kungsleden, was populated exclusively by Sámi until the beginning of the 19th century when agriculturalists arrived and established the first farm in 1827. Farming was viable on account of the lakes flooding every spring and naturally fertilising the surrounding fields. Hay was important, as witnessed at Aitenjas; many hay barns are preserved to this day on and close to the delta lands surrounding Ammarnäs. At this latitude, frost was a real problem for arable farming and the locals came up with the novel solution of planting on the inclined slopes of small hills formed of glacial deposits. Potatisbacke (potato hill) within the town itself is still planted to this day and is well worth a visit, as is the beautiful amber-coloured wooden church of 1858. Today, Ammarnäs's permanent population numbers around 120 although this is

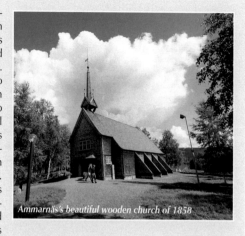

Ammarnäs's beautiful wooden church of 1858

swelled all year – by skiers in winter and tourists and walkers in summer. There is no bank or ATM in Ammarnäs, although cashback can be obtained at the Livs store. Cards are accepted in all outlets.

Naturum/tourist information
One of the first facilities encountered on entering Ammarnäs, the Naturum is a visitor centre for the Vindelälven Naturreservat which doubles as the town's tourist information centre. Opening hours are 0900–1100 and 1200–1700 daily and also 1900–2100 on Wednesday evenings. A notice board outside by the entrance has bus timetables, weather forecasts and other useful information. Inside there is an information desk manned by knowledgeable and helpful staff as well as a shop selling guidebooks, maps, postcards and souvenirs. Rubbing shoulders with the shop is a permanent and comprehensive exhibition about Vindelälven. Those walking northwards and planning to use the Rävfallsstugan can obtain a key at the information desk (tel 0952 60165 or 010 2254586, naturum.ammarnas@lansstyrelson.se, www. ammarnasfjallen.com/naturum – Swedish only).

Livs supermarket
Livs is the only sizeable store in town and it has very helpful staff. Opening hours are 1000–1800 Monday to Thursday, 1000–2000 Friday, 0900–1500 Saturday and 1100–1600 Sunday. The store is well-stocked with both fresh

and packaged conventional foods as well as fruit, vegetables and dairy products. Dehydrated trekking food is sold, but the stock often runs out. Maps, gas, meths, batteries, ready meals, chocolates and cold drinks and beer can all be purchased in the store. Livs is a Bussgods agent and will hold walkers' parcels for no charge. The store also issues keys for the Rävfallsstugan. Cashback is available with no surcharge so long as you make a purchase in store. There is no limit, although cashback transactions are only undertaken towards the end of the store's opening hours.

Ammarnäs Garden

This is both hotel and hostel and is directly next door to the Naturum. Hotel rooms start at SEK985 for a single (including breakfast), SEK1390 for a double. Facilities include a bar, restaurant, Wi-Fi, *bastu* and an indoor pool. Across the road is the hostel annex which offers a clean, simple and cheaper self-catering option likely to be more popular with walkers. The hostel has a kitchen, showers, lounge and a drying room. All rooms are twin and have their own toilet. Costs are SEK350 per person (tel 0952 60003, www.ammarnasgarden.se/eng).

Ammarnäs Wärdshus

This clean, spacious and airy STF-affiliated hotel and hostel can be found on the road to the Potatisbacke. It is largely aimed at fishermen, although its convivial and relaxed atmosphere should prove popular with walkers. Twin rooms cost SEK670 (SEK335 each). Camping is SEK150 with the use of a *servishus* that includes showers, toilets and bastu. Its restaurant is open 0800–0930, 1200–1400 and 1800–2100. There is a bar on site and Wi-Fi. A shop sells dehydrated trekking food, gas, white gas and maps (tel 0952 60200 or 073 3761897, www.fishyourdream.com/en/locations/ammarnas).

Ammarnäs Guide Centre

The guide centre is central and close to the Naturum and offers a café serving burgers, salads and pasta (including vegetarian options); camping; Wi-Fi; a shop, bar and hostel. Open 0800 till late, last food 2100–2200. Camping is SEK150 per tent, including showers and access to mains electricity. Rooms cost SEK300 per person on a shared basis. Off-site self-catering cabins are also available. The shop has gas, maps, dehydrated trekking food and energy bars. Staff are friendly and the centre is the place where people go to socialise and hang out (tel 073 0847033, info@ammarnasguide.se, www.ammarnasguide.se/index-uk.php).

The view from the top of the Potatisbacke out across the delta hay meadows

Potatisbacke (potato hill)

This small hill sits within Ammarnäs, close to the *wärdshus*. Formed from glacial debris, the Potatisbacke is perfectly conical in shape and offers a bird's eye view of the extensive delta hay meadows and barns. The angled slopes offer increased solar energy to crops and it was thus exploited to maximise outputs in this, a region where arable farming was a borderline activity. Today it is still used for growing although not on a self-sufficient basis. A path around the rear allows access to the top where there is a picnic area and fire pit. Across the road and well worth a visit is the church: its wooden boarding glows richly like honey on a sunny day.

SECTION 5 –
AMMARNÄS TO
HEMAVAN

Fine views eastwards on Stage 25

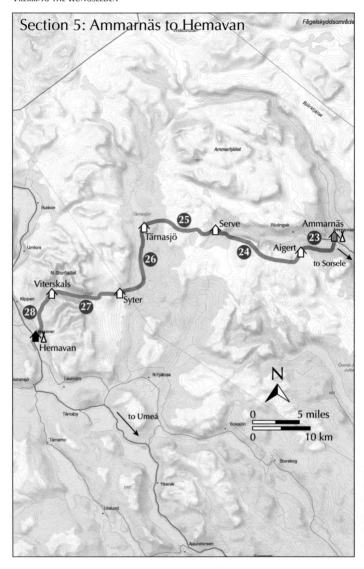

Section 5: Ammarnäs to Hemavan

SECTION 5

Ammarnäs to Hemavan

Start	Ammarnäs
Finish	Hemavan
Distance	77.1km (walking distance 77.1km)
Ascent	1875m
Descent	1745m
Terrain	Open fell and mountain, some forest
High point	Juovvatjåhkka Emergency Shelter 1070m (Stage 24)
Boat crossings	Optional: Stor-Tjulträsket

After the northern section between Abisko and Vakkotavare, this is the second most popular and well-trodden part of the Kungsleden although it's not all attributable to logistics. True, the entire section is furnished with regular STF *fjällstugor* and access, especially at Hemavan is very good. But what really draws people is

Big skies en route to Aigertstugan (Stage 23)

the grand finale of the Kungsleden, the unforgettable and spectacular transit of the Syterskalet glacial valley, a mere day before arriving at the finish in Hemavan. This is also the most varied section on the Kungsleden, encompassing forest, high fell plateau, fell meadows and a lakeside traverse. You will meet all manner of walkers en route to Hemavan from Ammarnäs; solo walkers, groups of friends and family groups, all making for a sociable atmosphere on the trail and at the *stugor*.

Save for a few limited kilometres, this, the newest section of the Kungsleden, is not marked with red paint as the others are. Marking is varied and consists of wooden poles, small rock cairns, slabs of rock positioned upright and winter markers. Signposting remains good and the trail is well delineated by the passage of feet.

Access

Ammarnäs lies at a roadhead and is linked to the outside world by the 341 bus service from Sorsele (70min). Sorsele can be accessed by buses 36 and 31 from Umeå or by the 45 bus from Arvidsjaur.

Hemavan is easily accessed, having an airport and a main road, though at present there are no scheduled flights. Hemavan is linked to Umeå by the 31 bus (five-and-a-half hours). From Umeå, SAS/Norwegian flights or SJ train can be used for onward travel to Stockholm.

Maps

- 1:75,000 Outdoorkartan Blad 6 (Ammarnäs-Hemavan-Lill-Björkvattnet) OR
- 1:100,000 Fjällkartan AC2 (Tärnaby-Hemavan-Ammarnäs) OR
- 1:100,000 Calazo Fjällkartor Vindelfjällen

STAGE 23
Ammarnäs to Aigert

Start	Ammarnäs 420m
Finish	Aigertstugan 790m
Distance	7.4km
Ascent	390m
Descent	20m
Grade	Easy
Time	3hr 10min
Terrain	Largely forest, some open fell towards the day's end
Shelter	Nil
Camping	Wild – nil. Paid – Aigert STF Fjällstuga
Resupply	Shop at Aigert STF Fjällstuga

This short day begins the final section of the Kungsleden and allows the options of either a late start or the opportunity to have a full day and push on beyond Aigert. The trail is not marked through Ammarnäs although it is easily picked up once out of town.

If short on time, it is possible to proceed direct to Servestugan (Stage 24's terminus) and save a day's walk. This is achieved by arranging a motorised boat to take you across Stor-Tjulträsket Lake and then walking the last 4km to Servestugan. When arranging the crossing, ask if it is possible for the boatman to give you a lift (8km) to where the boat departs from. This is a non-scheduled service, ask for boatmen's details at the Naturum in Ammarnäs. Costs are SEK560 if travelling alone or SEK280 per person when travelling in a group.

Head east from the Naturum and take the road bridge across to the south side of the **Tjulån River**. Pass the fire station and 50m further on, turn off right onto a gravel track at a Kungsleden sign. Soon the track divides, take the right-hand branch and continue for 15min to a

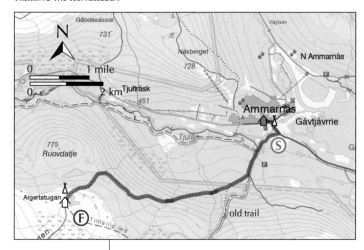

parking area where the route continues straight ahead as a dirt track. Follow this into the mixed forest to reach a latrine and signposts.

From the latrine, ascend along the narrow trail which has only winter markers at this point. After 20min walking, turn right at wooden signposts and follow red paint markers. The old route of the Kungsleden continued straight on at this point. Continue ascending along

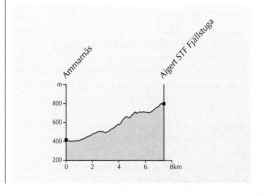

the rocky and root littered trail to arrive at another fork which is taken rightwards to a wooden bridge. A little further on cross a second such bridge which spans the Slagerbäcken River. Continue more steeply over a rocky and muddy trail to a third wooden bridge and the Ruovdatjjuhka River which spills and roars over a 4m step before disappearing through a narrow fissure into a gorge. ▸ Continue steeply for 15min before the trail relents. Continue ascending more gently and then along an undulating treeless and open section that affords great views down into the valley.

The forest is now birch only and will feel lighter and airy.

Traverse an area of marsh along boardwalks and a couple of wooden bridges. ▸ Once past the marsh, climb steeply via more boards and muddy trail onto a shoulder from where Ruovdatjjávrrie Lake will be seen nestling in the forest below. Reach the treeline once again just before cresting the shoulder and from the apex, Aigert STF Fjällstuga (**Aigertstugan**) will be seen 500m easy walk away. Those wishing to wild camp will find limited camp spots just prior to reaching the *stuga*.

This marshy area is rich in cloudberry.

The Ruovdatjjuhka tumbles over a 4m step

AIGERT STF FJÄLLSTUGA (790M)

Aigert STF Fjällstuga seen from the east

This *fjällstuga* stands on a rocky rise overlooking a small lake and commands great views of the mountains and trail that lie ahead. The *fjällstuga* was inaugurated in 1983 following much deliberation as to the exact routing the Kungsleden should take between Ammarnäs and Hemavan. Today there are beds for 26, including eight in a separate building for those walking with dogs. Camping is limited by the local terrain and most choose spots close to the lake (Ruovdatjjávrátje). The *fjällstuga* is well equipped with *bastu*, spacious communal area and a shop (snacks, trekking food, gas, meths, and drinks). Cards are accepted, as are Norwegian Krone and Euro. The notice boards include bus information (Ammarnäs–Sorsele) and the entire site has good phone signal which means that Swish – a mobile payment app popular in Sweden – can also be used for payments.

STAGE 24
Aigert to Serve

Start	Aigertstugan 790m
Finish	Servestugan 710m
Distance	19.2km
Ascent	575m
Descent	655m
Grade	Challenging
Time	6hr 30min
Terrain	Open fell with forest to finish
Shelter	Emergency shelters at Juovvatjåhkka and Vuomatjåhkka
Camping	Wild – many opportunities on the open fell. Paid – Serve STF Fjällstuga
Resupply	Shop at Serve STF Fjällstuga

This will feel like a long and rugged day spent traversing a barren high fell plateau, with very much a mountainous feel to the terrain. Two emergency shelters offer security for those making this high crossing in poor weather.

Head southwards from Aigert and traverse an area of marshy ground. Once through the marsh, begin a long gentle climb up the open fell following winter and stone markers. Good camp spots will be found besides a stream just prior to reaching a moraine bank. Continue more steeply as the pass between **Uhtsa-Áigart** (1076m) and **Dåriestjåhkka** (1157m) is approached and more steeply again as the path swings to the right for the final section of the climb. ▶ From the pass, traverse westwards across a rocky and barren plateau landscape passing lakes and knolls en route. Pass Tjålmure Lake noting the reindeer herder's cabin on an isthmus. Camping is possible almost anywhere up here, although it would be a harsh prospect in poor weather. Continue in a similar manner (following winter markers and red paint) for almost a further 3km to the emergency shelter

Snow patches remain in this area throughout the summer.

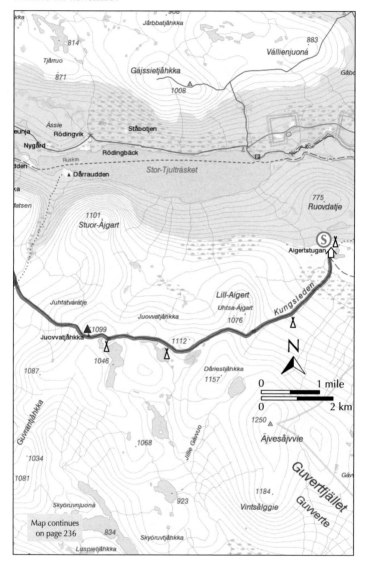

Map continues
on page 236

234

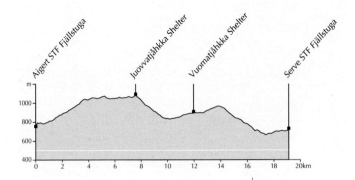

at **Juovvatjåhkka** which will hove into view silhouetted against the sky.

> Juovvatjåhkka emergency shelter (1070m) – this simple wooden cabin with a separate latrine stands exposed to the elements on the plateau's edge. A small entrance hall keeps the elements at bay from the main room which contains a small table, two sleeping platforms and a wood stove. Emergency firewood is provided as are blankets, an emergency radio and a *nödlåda*. Access to the *nödlåda* (a box containing emergency rations) is only by way of a key that is contained behind glass that must be broken; instructions for reporting broken key glass are provided. There is no phone signal. The shelter rather curiously has a ladder fixed against the outside next to the window. One can only conclude that this is to allow exit should the main door be blocked by heavy snowfall.

Begin descending immediately on leaving the shelter with expansive views ahead across the fells. A pair of red painted crosses indicate that **the paint markers are about to cease**. Continue the pleasant descent to level out at a junction just before the Gårssajuhka River, continue

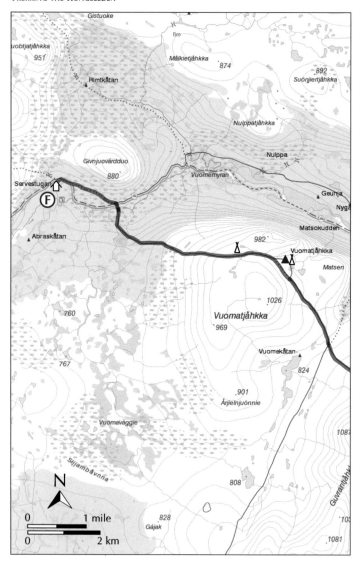

straight on and make the gentle, although sometimes muddy, ascent to a second emergency shelter.

> Vuomatjåhkka emergency shelter (860m) – this shelter is located 200m off the trail overlooking a small lake. Although of a *prisma* design, the interior and equipment are almost identical to the previous shelter, save for there being no emergency radio, phone signal being available on the high ground surrounding the shelter. Good camp spots are to be found in the area. On a clear day, Juovvatjåhkka shelter can be seen on the skyline.

Continue gently ascending from the shelter and 30min later cross through an ill-defined pass. Descend from the pass and before very long enter the birch tree-line. Soon the Servvejuhka River will be heard up ahead where it roars over a large cascade. Cross the wooden suspension bridge to the north bank and follow the rather muddy trail west for a final 2km of steady ascent to Serve STF Fjällstuga (**Servestugan**).

SERVE STF FJÄLLSTUGA (710M)

Serve STF Fjällstuga

This *stuga* occupies a compact clearing in the scant birch forest. There are beds for 22 and limited camp spots around the cabins; the best spot is out the back by a stream. There is a shop on site (cash only). Everyone shares the same communal area. Water at Serve should be boiled or sterilised. There is no *bastu*.

STAGE 25
Serve to Tärnasjö

Start	Servestugan 710m
Finish	Tärnasjöstugorna 610m
Distance	13.6km
Ascent	365m
Descent	465m
Grade	Easy
Time	4hr 50min
Terrain	Open fell with forest to finish
Shelter	Nil
Camping	Wild – many opportunities on the open fell. Paid – Tärnasjö STF Fjällstuga
Resupply	Shop at Tärnasjö STF Fjällstuga

The fells between Serve and Tärnasjö are very undemanding as well as being rich in flowers and other heath plants. This adds a meadow-like quality to the walk and is a distinct change to the high fell plateau of the previous day. Views will open up to the snow-flecked mountains that are the final barrier between you and the trail's end at Hemavan.

From Serve, resume heading westwards through the thinning birch and after 15min cross a wooden bridge. Exit the treeline and begin a 2km ascent to the pass south of **Servvetjåhkka** (967m). The climb is initially steep, although it eases after 20min. Red paint markers will give way to stone markers during the ascent to the pass. On reaching the pass good camp spots can be found close to some small pools. The view ahead will be into a large basin dominated by Servvejávrrie Lake and, in the far distance, a line of mountains splashed with patches of snow. ◄

A glance backwards reveals the fine sweeping curve of Suvlåjvvie (1352m).

Make a long and easy descent into the basin to reach a wooden bridge where the camping is very good. Continue easily on the gently undulating terrain passing

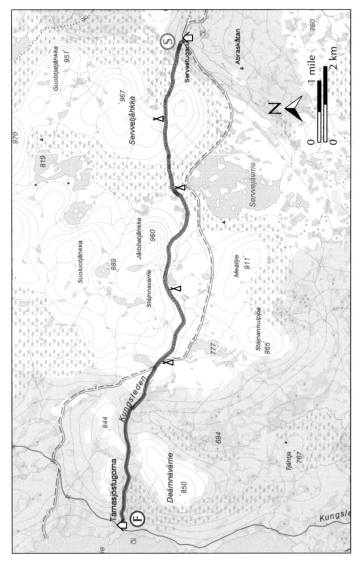

many camp spots as well as a rich variety of plants that include alpine flowers, crowberry, juniper and even ferns, the latter a rare sight on the Kungsleden. Climb out of the basin, finishing with a short, steeper section that reveals the first views of Tärnasjön Lake to the west. Follow the hillside via a small valley that is filled with birch and willow and delivers you to the attractive Siejdáge Lake.

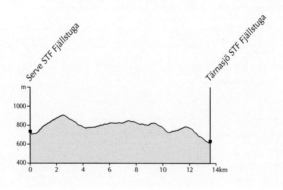

240

Camp spots can be found just before the birch and willow, the last good ones before Tärnasjöstugorna.

Descend from Siejdáge and enter the birch treeline. Continue heading downhill across firm ground and pass Tjärven Lake where, unfortunately, the ground is too boggy to camp. Climb gently for a short time and once past a small lake to the south, continue descending all the way to Tärnasjö STF Fjällstuga (**Tärnasjöstugorna**).

TÄRNASJÖ STF FJÄLLSTUGA (610M)

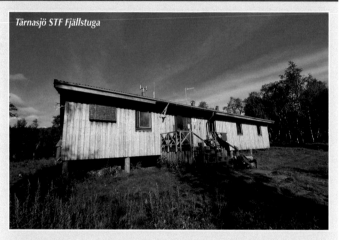

Tärnasjö STF Fjällstuga

Tärnasjöstugorna nestles in thin birch close to the shore of Tärnasjön. The present buildings were constructed in 1983/84 when the Kungsleden was being extended to Hemavan, although records exist back to 1922 of older buildings being used by walkers. Today the *stuga* is well equipped with a medium-sized shop and a *bastu* down by the lakeshore complete with a bucket shower. Tärnasjö does not accept bank cards. Camping is either by the lake or on good pitches 50m in front of the main building. There are beds for 26. Walkers with dogs are accommodated in a cabin closer to the lake, while campers use the spacious facilities of the main cabin. The site is not overly insect prone. Once again, walkers are advised to boil or treat their drinking water due to reported illness on this section of the trail.

STAGE 26
Tärnasjö to Syter

Start	Tärnasjöstugorna 610m
Finish	Syterstugan 710m
Distance	14.2km
Ascent	135m
Descent	35m
Grade	Moderate
Time	5hr
Terrain	Lakeside forest with open fell to finish
Shelter	Nil
Camping	Wild – some limited opportunities alongside Tärnasjön Lake. Paid – Syter STF Fjällstuga
Resupply	Shop at Syter STF Fjällstuga

The traverse of Tärnasjön's forested shoreline can feel somewhat enclosed and is in stark contrast to the open meadow feel of the previous day. A small archipelago at the lake's southern end adds some novelty before a final steep climb to Syter.

The trail is livened by a variety of flowers including *flädervänderot* (elder), *rödblära* (red campion) and *stormhatt* (storm hat) as well as cloudberry and angelica.

Depart Tärnasjö in a southerly direction close and parallel to the shoreline. The trail is both rocky and muddy in places but never excessively so. ◄ Continue for 4km and pass alongside a gravel beach with a small islet just offshore; a tiny camp spot and camp fire can be found just off the trail 100m short of the islet. Continue, bearing away from the water's edge and traverse a large open marshy area that allows views across the lake to N(ord) Sytertoppen (1768m) which is seen just peeping above the ridge of Skijrátjåhkka (1110m).

Continue to a second large open area consisting of scrub where poor camp spots can be found. From here you will be able to see and hear the roar of Rássjajuhkatje River crashing down the opposite hillside nearly 3km away. Continue southwards through alternating forest

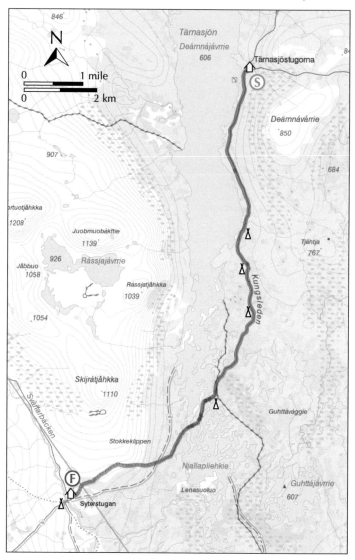

Gravel beach with Rássjatjåhkka on the far shore

Butterwort, a carnivorous plant, can be seen in these areas.

and clearings until a neglected **reindeer fence** is passed and very soon afterwards, reach the first of the bridges that span the archipelago to Tärnasjön's west shore. ◄ A very scruffy camp spot can be found just prior to this first bridge. Continue onwards, island hopping via a total of seven, sometimes wobbly, bridges.

Once across the bridges, continue easily through alternating forest and open areas until the trail begins to climb steeply under the watchful prow of Stokkeklippen. Emerge from the treeline and 400m further on reach the

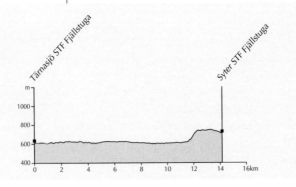

top of the climb. Looking backwards reveals the true complexity of the archipelago mosaic that was crossed earlier, ahead, Sjul-Olsaxeln juts from N Syttertoppen like a rampart. ▶ Follow the contour of the hillside comfortably, sometimes on boardwalks, until Syter STF Fjällstuga (**Syterstugan**) comes into view; 15min easy descent sees you there. There are no camp spots on this final section to the *stuga* and those wishing to wild camp are best continuing to the area southwest (and just across the bridge) from the buildings.

The distinct flowers of *Kung Karls spira* are seen along this section of trail.

SYTER STF FJÄLLSTUGA (710M)

Syter STF Fjällstuga catching some late-afternoon sunshine

Syterstugan commands a fantastic position besides the river Svärfarbäcken and looks up towards the high mass of N Syttertoppen; S(öder) Syttertoppen (1685m) remains largely obscured for the time being by Sjul-Olsaxeln. Although it is normal practice for *stugvärdar* to rotate around the *stugor* each season, Margared has been coming to Syter for over 20 years; needless to say, she is the font of all knowledge about the area.

Syter has beds for 28, 20 in the main cabin and another eight, for those with dogs, located in a cabin that dates back to 1926. Campers share the facilities of the main cabin and pitch outside or down by the river. Syter has a shop (cards accepted) and a *bastu*. Weather forecasts are available, although the site does also receive phone signal. There have been no reports of water problems at Syter and boiling water is not thought necessary.

STAGE 27
Syter to Viterskals

Start	Syterstugan 710m
Finish	Viterskalsstugan 800m
Distance	12.4km
Ascent	280m
Descent	190m
Grade	Moderate
Time	4hr 30min
Terrain	Open fell and glacial valley
Shelter	Emergency shelter at Syterskalet
Camping	Wild – many opportunities. Paid – Viterskals STF Fjällstuga
Resupply	Shop at Viterskals STF Fjällstuga

This stage is dominated by the walk through the mighty and impressive Syterskalet glacial valley. This is an archetypal u-shaped valley and one can only guess at the great powers that carved this deep channel through the high mountains. Rain or shine, a transit of the Syterskalet is always an uplifting experience.

Leave Syter via the wooden suspension bridge that spans the **Svärfarbäcken** and begin the long ascent of the open northeast flank of **Sjul-Olsaxeln**. The climb is steep initially but soon gives way and settles into a more comfortable gradient over good ground. Take two small wooden bridges that are followed by a short-lived steepening. Continue and level out on a broad and exposed saddle that lies between Sjul-Olsaxeln and **Vuekienaesie** (1012m), 1hr 40min from Syter. From here the distinct u-shape of Syterskalet begins to take form, the 'Sytertoppens' standing guard each side like the sentinels they are. Out on the bare saddle the vegetation is extremely short-cropped by the winds.

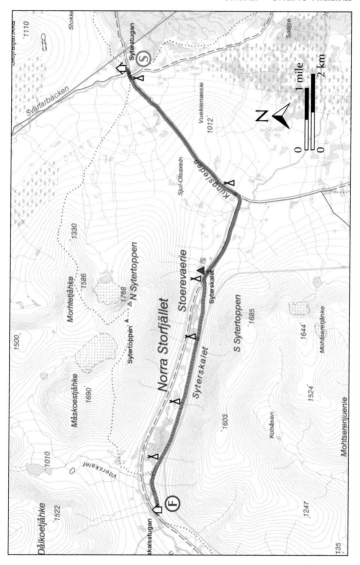

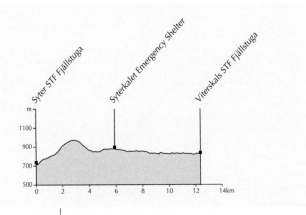

Syter STF Fjällstuga

Syterkalet Emergency Shelter

Viterskals STF Fjällstuga

Traverse the flat saddle taking boards where it is boggy. Descend easily off the high ground to ever improving views into Syterskalet. Nearing the bottom of the descent, there are camp spots protected to some extent by small banks. Continue to a signpost and swing right across boggy ground. A step in the trail signifies the

Looking back east along the Syterskalet

start of the gentle ascent to the shelter at the entrance to **Syterskalet** where there are camp spots.

Syterskalet emergency shelter (870m) – this shelter stands on the watershed at Syterskalet's eastern entrance and as such, can be an extremely windy and exposed spot. The shelter consists of a wooden cabin with an entrance hall and a main room. It is provided with a pair of wooden benches, a small table, wood stove, emergency wood, a *nödlåda* and emergency telephone. Outside there are a pair of latrines and nearby, a locked red reindeer-herder's cabin.

Leave the shelter and pick up the trail again as it begins its northwesterly transit of the valley south of the Syterbäcken River and under the dark cliffs, cirques, hanging streams and scree fans of **S Sytertoppen**. Continue along the valley floor, passing innumerable possible camp spots – although few offer shelter from the wind. The trail throughout is in good condition, neither boggy nor overly rocky and good time can be made. ▸ Small rock cairns mark the trail throughout the **Syterskalet**. Having walked 6km from the emergency shelter, start to make a long, slow sweep leftwards opposite the point where the **Viterskalet Valley** starts to appear. Here the Syterskalet is wider, less steep and less imposing. Pass a wooden bridge that leads to N Syttertoppen's summit (6km) via a trail marked with yellow rocks. Ahead, the dark buildings of Viterskals STF Fjällstuga (**Viterskalsstugan**) will be seen peeking above a shallow ridge 15min walk away.

The best views are back towards the shelter where the valley makes a perfect u-shape against the sky.

VITERSKALS STF FJÄLLSTUGA (800M)

Occupying a compact and seemingly solitary location, Viterskals literally straddles the Kungsleden by having a cabin two metres each side of the trail. There are beds for 24 and, uniquely for the Kungsleden, the *stuga* has a *tvättrum* (washroom) which is furnished with basins, a bucket shower and a warm stove flue; it is fantastic and more than makes up for there not being a *bastu* on site! Campers share facilities and can pitch at will; the best pitches

The compact Viterskals STF Fjällstuga

being 25m on the Hemavan side of the cabins, or just uphill of the cabins by the flagpoles. The shop accepts cards, as well as Norwegian Krone and Euro, if the *stugvärd* is not around an honesty system is in operation. The site is windy and therefore not prone to insects. There is no phone signal at Viterskals, although Västerbotten bus timetables and weather forecasts are posted. There are no reported water problems at the *stuga*.

STAGE 28
Viterskals to Hemavan

Start	Viterskalsstugan 800m
Finish	Hemavan 550m
Distance	10.3km
Ascent	130m
Descent	380m
Grade	Easy
Time	4hr
Terrain	Open fell, forest to finish
Shelter	Open-sided shelter above Hemavan
Camping	Wild – many opportunities on the open fell. Paid – Hemavan
Other accommodation	Many options in Hemavan
Resupply	Hemavan

A short and easy stage to finish the Kungsleden accompanied by views out across the low-lying forest and lakes of the Umeälven Valley. Hemavan has an airport, although bus and train will see onward travellers in Stockholm by early next morning. Those starting the Kungsleden from Hemavan will be able to source much of what they require locally, although dehydrated trekking food is difficult to find.

Follow the trail which remains elevated above the V Syterbäcken River so as to avoid marshy ground. ▶ Continue easily down the valley and after 4km, reach a signpost and a latrine. A wooden suspension bridge crosses the V Syterbäcken at this point. **Do not cross the bridge**, but instead follow the Hemavan sign and climb up the hillside where faint red paint markers start to make a reappearance. Level out besides another signpost where there is sufficient space and level ground for a few tents to be pitched. Continue ascending a short distance before levelling out and making a long undulating traverse across the hillside; there are many

The Syterskalet by now has lost all its steep brooding grandeur to become wide and easy angled.

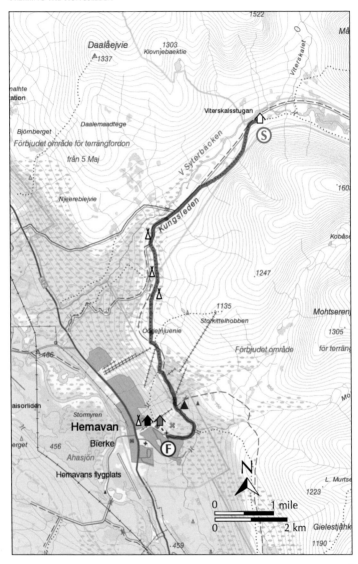

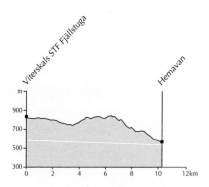

potential camp spots with long views out across the forests and lakes of the Umeälven Valley.

On reaching a knoll, traverse it via its east flank and take in the first proper views down onto Hemavan. Descend off the knoll following orange paint markers and enter the thin birch treeline. Follow the undulating trail that crosses a bridge near a ski tow and then pass an

First sight of Hemavan down in the Umeälven Valley

253

open-sided shelter (660m and some 100m off to the left of the trail). Continue through the trees following signs and markers which, at the end of a long rightwards swing of the trail, bring you to a large wooden sign that marks the end of the Kungsleden.

HEMAVAN (550M)

This small ski resort caters mostly for the domestic market as well as being popular with Norwegians and Finns. In summer it is rather quiet and although it seems large, it has only a few hundred permanent residents. The E12 road passes through Hemavan and allows good access by road in and out. An airport handles mainly ski charter flights in the winter although no scheduled flights serve the resort in the summer season. For those starting the Kungsleden in Hemavan, a number of shops and stores ensure that most trekkers' needs are met although dehydrated trekking rations are not always available. Bank cards can be used everywhere and an ATM is also available. There are a large number of accommodation options available in town.

Naturum

This visitor centre is located at the Kungsleden's terminus and is unmissable on account of its golden orb tower. The helpful staff can provide detailed information on all of Hemavan's facilities and the shop stocks maps and guides. The centre is part of the Vindelälven Naturreservat and accordingly has a permanent exhibition similar to that found in Ammarnäs. Located alongside the Naturum is the Fjällbotaniska (mountain plants) which exhibits the fell and mountain plants indigenous to the region. Those starting their walk from Hemavan are thus able to get a good introduction to the plants they will encounter on their journey northwards. The Naturum is at the very top of Hemavan, all other services and facilities are down below in the town itself (tel 0954 38023 or 070 3938023, naturum.hemavan@lansstyrelsen.se, www.hemavantarnaby.com/en/).

Hemavan Fjällstation

Centrally located, this clean, large and comfortable STF-affiliated hostel consists of a two-storey main building and a single-storey annex with beds for 90. Camping is available and facilities are shared with those staying in the annex. The hostel has a *bastu* and also a small shop selling gas, meths, white gas and sometimes, dehydrated trekking food. Bank cards are accepted

The unmistakable Naturum at the trail's end

and non-guests can use the showers for SEK20. Reception is open between 0800–1100 and 1600–2000 daily. STF members can use the kitchen for free on the normal day-visitor basis, although using the washing machine costs . There is no bar on site (tel 0954 30027, info@hemavanfjallstation.se, www. hemavanfjallstation.se – Swedish only).

Hemavan Fjällcenter
A second STF-affiliated hostel although seemingly less popular with walkers. This hostel and hotel is located close to the airport and has bed and self-catering space for 200 as well as camping facilities. There is also Wi-Fi, a bar (1700–2300), restaurant, *bastu* and an indoor swimming pool on site. STF members can use the kitchen for free on the normal day-visitor basis. The fjällcenter also sells maps and guides (0954 30002, info@hemavansfjall-center.se, www.hemavansfjallcenter.se/?lang=en).

Shops
Located on the main E12 road, a modest-sized shopping centre contains a self-service restaurant and an ICA supermarket as well as having an ATM. The ICA is open daily 0900–2100 and contains a good choice and range of conventional food, although it sells neither fuel nor dehydrated trekking food.

Across the road from the shopping centre, Ingo petrol station (open 24hrs) is next door to the Jarnia hardware store, which sells gas, meths and white gas as well as batteries and hardware. Jarnia opens weekdays 0700–1700, Saturday 0900–1500 and is closed Sunday.

Restaurants
Nannas Kök (Nanna's Kitchen) is a popular and modern licenced restaurant located close to the shopping centre and is open from 1600 Monday to Friday, from 1200 on Saturday and from 1600 on Sunday (tel 0954 30111, info@nannaskok.se, www.nannaskok.se – Swedish only).

Kungsporten is a fast-food restaurant located towards the airport offering kebabs, burgers, pizza and soft drinks. It is a Bussgods agent.

ONWARD TRAVEL

The efficient number 31 bus service links Hemavan with Umeå to the east from where you can join the main SJ rail network. Afternoon departures arrive in time to catch the SJ night train to Stockholm (departing Umeå 2155 and arriving Stockholm Central 0630).The 131 bus departs from outside the shopping centre. Be sure to check timetables for seasonal variations and exact times (www.tabussen.nu/lanstrafiken/english (buses) and www.sj.se/en/home.html (SJ trains)).

APPENDIX A
Summary of facilities

Location	Main accommodation	Shop	Beds	Bastu	Bank cards accepted	Phone signal	Notes
Abisko	STF *fjällstation*, many other accommodation options	large	100+	yes	yes	yes	large shop offering parcel holding, petrol station
Abiskojaure	STF *fjällstuga*	large	61	yes	yes	no	
Alesjaure	STF *fjällstuga*	large	86	yes	yes	no	
Tjäktja	STF *fjällstuga*	no	20	no	yes	no	
Sälka	STF *fjällstuga*	large	53	yes	yes	no	
Singi	STF *fjällstuga*	no	49	no	yes	no	
Kaitumjaure	STF *fjällstuga*	large	30	yes	yes	no	
Teusajaure	STF *fjällstuga*	large	30	yes	yes	no	
Vakkotavare	STF *fjällstuga*	medium	18	no	yes	yes	
Saltoluokta	STF *fjällstation*	large	100	yes	yes	no	parcel holding
Sitojaure	STF *fjällstuga*	no	18	no	yes	yes	some basic supplies available from Lars and Anna Blind who operate the lake crossing
Aktse	STF *fjällstuga*	large	34	yes	yes	no	
Pårte	STF *fjällstuga*	no	26	no	no	no	

Location	Main accommodation	Shop	Beds	Bastu	Bank cards accepted	Phone signal	Notes
Kvikkjokk	STF *fjällstation*, free camping	large	60	yes	yes	yes	parcel holding and cashback
Tsielekjåkkå	unmanned STF *stuga* (very basic)	no	4 (on wooden sleeping benches)	no	n/a	no	
Stage 15	*kåta* (very basic turf shelter)	no	4 (on earth floor)	no	n/a	no	
Vuonatjviken	self-catering, free camping	very basic shop	groups of up to 10	no	yes	yes	
Jäkkvik	Kyrkans Fjällgård (hostel), paid camping, other self-catering options available	large	80	yes	yes	yes	Handlar'n shop offering parcel holding and cashback, petrol station
Pieljekaise	unmanned non-STF *stuga*	no	4 (bunks with mattresses)	no	no	no	collect key in Jäkkvik or Adolfsström
Adolfsström	various self-catering options, paid camping	large	many	yes	yes	yes	large shop, petrol station, tourist information
Bäverholmen	*värdshus*, paid camping	no	20	no	yes	yes	restaurant
Snjultjie	basic cabin	no	(narrow wooden sleeping benches)	no	no	no	

Location	Main accommodation	Shop	Beds	*Bastu*	Bank cards accepted	Phone signal	Notes
Rävfalls	unmanned non-STF *stuga*	no	14 (bunks with mattresses, pillows and blankets)	yes	no	no	collect key in Adolfsström or Ammarnäs
Ammarnäs	many options: hostel, hotel, self-catering, STF-affiliated *fjällstation*, paid camping	large	many	yes	yes	yes	large shop (Livs) offering parcel holding and cashback, petrol station, bars and restaurants, tourist information, parcel holding at *fjällstation*
Aigert	STF *fjällstuga*	medium	26	yes	yes	yes	
Serve	STF *fjällstuga*	medium	22	no	no	yes	
Tärnasjö	STF *fjällstuga*	medium	26	yes	no	no	
Syter	STF *fjällstuga*	medium	28	yes	yes	yes	
Viterskals	STF *fjällstuga*	medium	24	no	yes	no	
Hemavan	STF affiliated *fjällstationer*, many other accommodation options	large	290	yes	yes	yes	parcel holding at *fjällstationer*, shopping centre with large grocery store, ATM, bars and restaurants, fast food, cafés, petrol station, tourist information, airport
Kebnekaise	STF *fjällstation*	large	100+	yes	yes	yes	parcel holding
Nikkaluokta	Sarri AB	small	6-bed houses	yes	yes	yes	camping

APPENDIX B
Useful contacts

The dialling code for Sweden is +46

Swedish Tourist Association (STF)
website
(information on the Kungsleden,
STF membership and accommodation
booking)
www.swedishtouristassociation.com

Transport

Rail
Swedish Railways (SJ)
www.sj.se/en/home.html

Inlandsbanan
(regional trains)
www.inlandsbanan.se/en

Bus
Länstrafiken Norrbotten
(local bus services in
Norrbotten county)
www.ltnbd.se/en/timetables

Länstrafiken Västerbotten
(local bus services in
Västerbotten county)
www.tabussen.nu/lanstrafiken/english

Hörvalls Nikkaluoktaexpressen
(privately operated bus from
Kiruna to Nikkaluokta)
www.horvalls.se
(Swedish only)

Air
SAS Airlines
www.flysas.com/en/uk

Norwegian Air
www.norwegian.com/uk

Regional Jet (Nordica)
www.nordica.ee/en/home

Accommodation
For *fjällstation* and *fjällstuga* bookings
fjallbokningen@stfturist.se

Abisko STF Fjällstation
tel 0980 40200

Kebnekaise STF Fjällstation
tel 0980 55000
kebnekaise@stfturist.se

Saltoluokta STF Fjällstation
tel 010 1902350

Kvikkjokk STF Fjällstation
tel 0971 21022
info@kvikkjokkfjallstation.se

Vuonatjviken
tel 073 0358673 or 070 6968045
eva@vuonatjviken.com

Bäverholms Värdshus
tel 0961 23018
baverholmsvardshus@hotmail.se

Hemavan STF Fjällstation
tel 0954 30027
info@hemavanfjallstation.se

Hemavan STF Fjällcenter
tel 0954 30002
info@hemavansfjallcenter.se

Parcel holding
Bussgods
www.bussgods.se
(Swedish only)

Weather
To calculate day length
www.suncalc.net

For historical climate graphs
www.wunderground.com/history

Maps
Lantmäteriet Sverige
(online mapping resources)
www.lantmateriet.se/en/

Stanfords
www.stanfords.co.uk

The Map Shop
www.themapshop.co.uk

Other
Swedish Ornithological Society
www.birdlife.se
(Swedish only)

APPENDIX C

Summary of boat crossings

Current information and tariffs can be found on a dedicated STF webpage: www.swedishtouristassociation.com/learn/boats-in-the-mountains

Crossing	Crossing Status	Stage	Distance (km)	STF rowing boats	Motorised service	Cost (SEK)	Contact details
Alisjávri	Optional	2	5.0	No	Yes – private	350	-
Teusajaure	Mandatory	8	1.0	Yes	Yes – STF	100/150	-
Langas	Mandatory	8	3.5	No	Yes – STF	120/180	-
Sitojaure	Mandatory	10	3.6	Yes	Yes – private	300	tel 073 0799603 or 010 4016347 or sitojaure@hotmail.com
Lájtávrre	Mandatory	11	3.0	Yes	Yes – STF and private	200	-
Sakkat	Mandatory	13	2.7	No	Yes – private	200	tel 070 2053193 or 073 8006232
Riebnes	Mandatory	17	6.0	No	Yes – private	350	tel 073 0358673, 070 6968045 or eva@vuonatjviken.com
Harrselet-Härresavvun	Mandatory	17	0.4	Yes	No	-	-
Iraft	Optional	19	5.0	No	Yes	150–300	tel 0961 23018
Stor-Tjulträsket	Optional	23 and 24	5.0	No	Yes	280–560	-
Láddjujávri	Optional	Additional itinerary 1	7.0	No	Yes	350	tel 073 031 70 27, 070 535 56 66 or info@enoks.se

The dialling code for Sweden is +46

APPENDIX D
Language

Although the vast majority of Swedish people speak very good English, it is always useful and respectful to have some words and phrases in the local dialect, be it Swedish or Fell (Northern) Sámi. Walkers will also find it helpful if they have a grasp of the written Swedish word where it appears on local bus timetables, notices and information boards. A great many geographical features on mapping are labelled in Sámi. In the following table, phonetic pronunciation is shown in brackets.

Salutations

English	Swedish	Fell Sámi
Hello	Hej [hey]	Bures
Goodbye	Hej då [hey daw]	Mana dearvan – to person leaving, Báze dearvan – to person staying
Yes	Ja [yaa]	De lea
No	Nej [ney]	Li
Please	Tack [tak]	Leage buorre
Thank you	Tack [tak]	Giitu
Thank you very much	Tack så mycket [tak saw me-ke]	Ollu giitu
You're welcome	Varsågod [var-sha-gohd]	Leage buorre
Sorry	Förlåt [feur-lawt]	Ándagassii
Excuse me	Ursäkta mig [oor-shek-ta mey]	Maid lohket
How are you?	Hur mår du? [hoor mawr doo]	Got manna?/Mii gallo?

Mapping and geographic

English	Swedish	Fell Sámi
North	Norr	
South	Söder [su-der]	
East	Öster [es-ter]	
West	Väster [ves-ter]	
Lake	Sjö [s-yo]	Jaure, jávri [yow-re] or láhko

English	Swedish	Fell Sámi
River	Flod	Jokk
Brook	Bäck	Johka
Bridge	Bro [brooo]	Saldi
Path/road	Väg [veg]	Rátti
Mountain	Berg [berry] or fjäll [fy-al]	Várri
Glacier	Glaciär, jökel	Jiehkki
Peak	Fjälltopp	Čohkka
Valley	Dal [dahl], dalen or dalgång	Vagge or vaggi
Boat crossing	Båtled [bot-lyed]	
Mountain station	Fjällstation	
Mountain hut	Fjällstuga	
Reindeer enclosure	Rengärde [reen-yard-e]	
Ravine(s)	Ravin[er]	
Dilapidated/ruined	Förfallen	

Travel and Timetables

English	Swedish	Fell Sámi
Boat	Båt [baw-t]	
Bus	Buss [bu-s]	
Bus station	Busstation [boos-sta-hoon]	
Aeroplane	Flygplan [fleeg-plaa-n]	
Airport	Flygplats [fleeg-plats]	
Train	Tåg [taw-g]	
Train station	Tågstation [tawg-sta-hoon]	
First	Först [feursh-t]	
Last	Sist [sis-t]	
Next	Nästa [nes-ta]	
One-way ticket	Enkelbiljett [en-kel-bil-yet]	
Return ticket	Returbiljett [re-toor-bil-yet]	
Depart	Avresa [av-ree-esa]	

English	Swedish	Fell Sámi
Departure	Avgång [av-gong]	
Arrival	Ankomst [an-com-st]	
Delayed	Försenad [fu-she-an-ad]	
Cancelled	Avbokad [av-boo-ked]	
Change	Ändra [and-dra]	
Open	Öppet [up-et]	Rabas
Closed	Stängd [st-aay-nd]	
Only	Endast [end-ust]	
Every	Varge [var-ye]	
To/Until	Till [t-eel]	
From	Från [fr-on]	
Between	Mellan [mel-lon]	Gaska

Times

English	Swedish	Fell Sámi
Day	Dag [darg]	Beaivi
Daily	Daglig [dag lig]	
Week	Vecka [vek-ya]	Vahkku
Weekly	Vecko [vek-oh]	
Month	Månad [maw-nad]	Mánnu
Monday	Måndag [mawn-daa]	Mánnodat
Tuesday	Tisdag [tees-taa]	Disdat
Wednesday	Onsdag [ohns-daa]	Gaskavahku
Thursday	Torsdag [torsh-daa]	Duorastat
Friday	Fredag [frey-daa]	Bearjadat
Saturday	Lördag [leur-daa]	Lávvordat
Sunday	Söndag [seun-daa]	Sotnabeaivi/Bassi
Today	Idag [ee-daa]	Odne
Yesterday	Igår [ee-gawr]	
Tomorrow	Imorgon [ee-mor-ron]	

Fjällstugor and fjällstationer

English	Swedish
Water	Vatten
Toilet/privvy	Dass
Wood	Ved
Waste water	Slask
Sauna	Bastu
Warden	Stugvärd
Boil	Koka
Urinal	Pissoar
Service cabin (campers)	Tältservicestuga
Emergency telephone	Hjälptelefon
Shop	Butik
Emergency room	Säkerhetsrum
Garbage	Sopor
Laundry	Tvätt
Washroom	Tvättrum
Service house	Servishus
Edible	Ätbart
Drying room	Torkrum
Breakfast	Frukost
Lunch	Lunch
Dinner	Middag
Camping area	Tältplatser
Main building	Huvud byggnad
Rowing boat	Roddbåt
No dogs	Ej hundar
Emergency box	Nödlåda
Vacant	Ledigt
Occupied	Upptaget
Member	Medlem

The hay meadows at Aktse (Stage 10)

DOWNLOAD THE ROUTES
IN GPX FORMAT

All the routes in this guide are available for download from:

www.cicerone.co.uk/982/GPX

as GPX files. You should be able to load them into most formats of mobile device, whether GPS or smartphone.

When you go to this link, you will be asked for your email address and where you purchased the guide, and have the option to subscribe to the Cicerone e-newsletter.

www.cicerone.co.uk

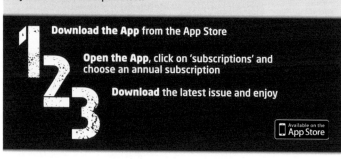

LISTING OF CICERONE GUIDES

For full information on all our guides,
books and eBooks,
visit our website:
www.cicerone.co.uk

Walking – Trekking – Mountaineering – Climbing – Cycling

Over 40 years, Cicerone have built up an outstanding collection of over 300 guides, inspiring all sorts of amazing adventures.

Every guide comes from extensive exploration and research by our expert authors, all with a passion for their subjects. They are frequently praised, endorsed and used by clubs, instructors and outdoor organisations.

All our titles can now be bought as **e-books**, **ePubs** and **Kindle** files and we also have an online magazine – **Cicerone Extra** – with features to help cyclists, climbers, walkers and trekkers choose their next adventure, at home or abroad.

Our website shows any **new information** we've had in since a book was published. Please do let us know if you find anything has changed, so that we can publish the latest details. On our **website** you'll also find great ideas and lots of detailed information about what's inside every guide and you can buy **individual routes** from many of them online.

It's easy to keep in touch with what's going on at Cicerone by getting our monthly **free e-newsletter**, which is full of offers, competitions, up-to-date information and topical articles. You can subscribe on our home page and also follow us on **Facebook** and **Twitter** or dip into our **blog**.

Cicerone – the very best guides for exploring the world.

CICERONE

Juniper House, Murley Moss, Oxenholme Road, Kendal, Cumbria LA9 7RL
Tel: 015395 62069 info@cicerone.co.uk
www.cicerone.co.uk